An Unlikely Hero

Steve Zimmerman

Published 2015
Printed in the United States of America
ISBN: 978-0-692-41645-7

Cover and interior design by Tabitha Lahr

Also by the author:

Food in the Movies

For my father, who would be pleased.

And for Jean, my first reader and editor,
whose keen insights and blue pencil helped
turn my memories into a book.

"Memories collect in us and form aquifers of meaning below the surface of our lives."

—Nuala O'Faolain, *Chicago Mary*

"I will cherish my visit here in memory for as long as I live."

—Audrey Hepburn in *Roman Holiday.*

"Manliness without ostentation I learnt from what I have heard and remembered of my father."

—Marcus Aurelius, *Meditations*

Prologue

"They don't make men like him anymore."

This is a phrase I sometimes heard when I was growing up in the Bronx in the 1940s, and I understood it to mean a man who possessed certain qualities: honesty, responsibility, generosity and integrity as well as a certain amount of insight into the human condition. In Yiddish, a *mensch*. In my father's case he acquired these qualities growing up on his own on the Lower East Side of New York at the turn of the twentieth century.

Sadly, I never heard anyone in my family speak of my father in this way during his lifetime. But there he was, an ordinary working man, proving his worth every day, and doing so without drawing attention to himself. Although his life was marked by unusual adversity, he met life's challenges gallantly in a calm, self-effacing manner, that deserves to be recognized by the phrase "They don't make men like him anymore."

My father was forty-seven when I was born, and, as is typical with most children, I showed little interest in his life before he met and married my mother. I rarely asked him questions about his life, about his growing-up years, his aspirations, his dreams, his disappointments. And I couldn't ask my mother about him since she died of brain cancer when I was six years old.

During the last eight years of my father's life I was either away from home serving in the Navy, or busy attending college. Had I been more mature, more sensitive, I could have found time to ask him about his life, and like most human beings, I'm certain he would have relished the chance to talk about his journey: to have someone, especially his son, listen to his stories and share his moments of happiness and bear witness to his hardships. Yes, there are some stories he passed on to me, but looking back now I realize they are far too few. There must have been much more to his life than I will ever know. It was a missed opportunity that I regret to this day. This book, then, is more than a memoir of my life growing up with my father. It is more than a family biography. It is, with the scant material at my disposal, an act of homage to the memory of my father, my unlikely hero.

Chapter One

Let me say at the outset, that it is impossible to write about my father without writing about myself and my family. I have tried to do this as honestly and as faithfully as my memory will allow. In each instance where the memory is about myself, I have tried to get it down on paper as I experienced it in the moment, not as I reflect on it now through a gauzy veil of time. Of course, what is important about memories, mine or anyone else's, is not how accurate they are, but the meaning they hold for the person who possesses them, and how that meaning gets woven into the fabric of our lives.

As with most life stories, I begin at the beginning when my parents first arrived in this country as part of the great migration to the Goldeneh Medinah, the Golden Land, which began with a trickle in 1881 and became a steady stream by 1906 when nearly two million Jews had left their homes. The majority of them settled on New York's Lower East Side, which soon became the world's largest Jewish community. They were not the only immigrants seeking refuge in America at this time. Millions of Italians, Irish and other immigrants arrived on the shores of America in the late 1880s through the first decades of the twentieth century, many of them, like the Jews, settling on the Lower East Side, and all of them finding one reason or another to dislike each other.

My father, Arthur Zimmerman, was born in 1886 and emigrated with his family from Kiev, Russia, to the United States sometime during the last decade of the 19th century. Kiev is located in the north central part of Russia on the Dnieper River in the Ukraine. Throughout its long history as one of Eastern Europe's oldest cities, it went through periods of economic prosperity followed by years of decline. Similarly, anti-Semitism also rose and declined over the centuries. By the 18th and 19th centuries Kiev was once again an important trade and transportation center with a sprawling railway system, and Jews had played a role in the city's recovery, plying their trade as merchants and money handlers. According to my father, it was also a city where horse thieves gathered.

When my father's family lived in Kiev, it was pretty much ruled by the Russian army in partnership with ecclesiastical authorities who, it would appear, grudgingly tolerated the presence of Jews. In 1881, triggered by increasing economic pressures, Czar Alexander lll imposed new restrictions on Russian Jews forbidding them to acquire land, establishing Jewish quotas in schools and universities, and instituting pogroms resulting in mass riots and the wholesale slaughter of Jews and looting of their property. Eight years later the government decreed that all Jews must leave Russia, initiating a mass exodus not witnessed since the departure of Jews from Egypt. This harsh treatment undoubtedly prompted my grandparents to flee for their lives. This was just as well, because in October, 1943, soon after the Russians recaptured Kiev from the Germans during World War II, the Soviet news agency TASS reported, reliably or not, that in 1941 the Germans had murdered all the Jews in Kiev in a matter of days.

In his scholarly book, *World of our Fathers*, Irving Howe documents the social and cultural history of Eastern European Jews who settled in America at the turn of the twentieth century. He records an eyewitness account of life on the Lower East Side of New York during this period. The picture he paints describes what my father must have experienced as a young boy newly arrived in the land of opportunity:

> Toilet facilities, two to a floor at best and foul privies at worst, allowing neither the simplicities of nature nor the convenience of civilization, added to the sense of people intolerably packed together. So did the clutter of buildings, the lack of ground space, the clamor of drays, refuse carts, grocery wagons. Perhaps worst was the assault of smells: the odors of human waste only intermittently carted away from back-yard privies by a careless sanitation department, the stench of fish and meat starting to rot on pushcarts, the foulness of neglected sewers and gutters. Life was abrasive, clamorous.

Upon arriving in this country my father's family settled on Hester Street, at the corner of Ludlow, which at the time was one of the chief market centers on the Lower East Side. It was a time when nearly fifty percent of all tenement households (regardless of ethnicity) slept three or four to a room, and twenty-five percent slept five or more in a room. The running joke among Jews was "Sleep quick, we need the pillows."

Hester Street lay in the center of what Jacob Riis, the celebrated New York newspaperman at the turn of the century, called "Jewtown." Like many other streets in this enclave, it was lined with pushcarts allowing barely enough room for "schleppers" and horse-drawn carriages to maneuver. Walking space for pedestrians on sidewalks was narrowed considerably by the presence of makeshift wooden stalls placed there by shop owners eager to snare the attention of shoppers. Only a few blocks from where my father lived was the Essex Street Market, another hectic trading area, where everything but a pig could be bought— peaches at a penny a quart, eyeglasses for thirty-five cents, old coats for fifty cents, oilcloth, garlic and much more. It was also a place where greenhorns would bunch up in the morning to wait for employers looking for cheap labor.

In the midst of this tumultuous commercial and residential milieu stood the imposing Ludlow Street county jail with eighty-seven cells, each ten feet square. Built during the Civil War, it primarily housed debtors. Its most celebrated guest was the notoriously corrupt politician William "Boss" Tweed who died there on April 12, 1878 at the age of fifty-five. Although the prison served as an ever-present visual reminder that "crime doesn't pay," it was not a message that all denizens and street urchins took to heart. The jail was bulldozed in the late 1920s.

For my father, as for many other ghetto children, life at home was not easy. There was constant friction as immigrant parents, bewildered by the bustling life they encountered in their new world, tried in vain to preserve Old World customs and religious beliefs, while their children were trying every which way to adapt to their new surroundings—and the streets were their school. In Howe's writings, he tells us that, "the streets were ours:"

Everyplace else—home, school, shop—belonged to the grownups. But the

> streets belonged to us . . . .The streets taught us the deceits of commerce, introduced us to the excitement of sex, schooled us in strategies of survival, and gave us our clear idea of what life in America was really going to be like…We might continue to love our parents and grind away at school and college, but it was the streets that prepared the future . . . Just to walk through Hester Street was an education in the hardness of life.

It's true, the streets were theirs, provided they didn't roam too far from their own neighborhoods. It was inevitable, I guess, whether out of curiosity or derring-do, that my father and his friends would cross the well-defined boundary lines that separated them from unfriendly gentile neighborhoods –like west of the Bowery where the Italians had settled, or beyond Cherry Street on the south where the Irish mostly resided. This was alien territory. It was where the *others* lived, and if one ventured onto these streets he had better be prepared for a fight, as my father obviously was. It was not uncommon, according to my father, for him and his friends to be the target of flying rocks and bricks, hurled by workers as they passed gentile lumberyards on the way to the East River for a swim (often in oil slick murky water) on a sultry summer day. (For fifty years or more, Irish immigrants often received similar threats and treatment from their natural enemies, the Nativists.) But more often my father and his cohorts were accosted by kids their own age who demanded money from these "Jew-boys." After repeated scuffles, my father told me he devised a plan that would allow him and his friends to outsmart their adversaries. He told each of his friends that when the Irish toughs approached them, and made them raise their hands above their heads so they could rifle their pockets for loose change, that that was the exact moment for them to start swinging at their unprotected faces. According to my father, his tactics worked as planned and he and his friends managed to send their assailants hightailing it to safety —at least on this occasion. If my father's story is accurate—and I believe it is, since I never knew him to indulge in self-aggrandizement, in my eyes he had shown a lot of moxie, and I remember how my childhood admiration for him had swelled.

My father, like many other Jewish kids on the Lower East Side, learned how to use his fists at an early age to protect himself. But there were other, much tougher Jewish kids who not only used their fists but also knives, bats and guns to pursue a life of crime in order to escape a life of poverty. The story of a group of such kids, learning their craft in the 1920s, is beautifully and graphically told in the uncut version of *Once Upon a Time in America* (d: Sergio Leone, 1984)starring Robert De Niro, James Woods and Elizabeth McGovern.

A poignant scene in this movie struck a nostalgic note in

me, because it had to do with a rich pastry dessert that was a favorite of mine when I was five or six years old living in the Bronx. In the film, these scamps, when not stealing or scrapping with other boys, often thought about girls, and particularly about having sex with them. This is the situation Patrick "Patsy" Goldberg (Brian Bloom), finds himself in. He is a pubescent Jewish *momzer* who figures he can get what he wants from Peggy (Amy Ryder), a neighborhood girl in her mid-teens who'll do anything with the boys for a charlotte russe. Before going to visit her, Patsy stops at "Fat Moe's" and buys one of these scrumptious desserts for five-cents. When a friend questions his extravagance, he replies, "For two pennies she only gives you a hand job. I can do that myself."

After he slicks down his hair, and hides his neatly wrapped payola behind his back, he knocks on Peggy's apartment door in a typical tenement. Her mother appears and tells him that Peggy is taking a bath and will be out soon. With nothing to do but wait, he sits on the top step just outside the front door to her apartment. Shortly, his attention focuses on the package he's holding. He sneaks a peek inside and, as if by accident, allows his finger to brush against the irresistible whipped cream topping which he licks clean.

Struggling against his conflicting desires, he slowly and carefully unties the string protecting his bait and spreads the wrapping paper out flat to get a full view of the delicacy he's safeguarding. Once again he runs his finger against the whipped topping before he attempts to re-wrap the pastry, which he is unable to do. By this time his appetite has gotten the upper hand, and he plucks the bright red cherry—perched on top of this creamy white mammary-like creation—and plop it in his mouth. His resistance grows ever weaker as he tries to decide which he wants more—the charlotte russe, or sex with Peggy. As he vacillates, he looks up at Peggy's door and then down at the charlotte russe. Suddenly his mind is made up, and he ravenously attacks the pastry dessert with both hands, licking his lips and fingers in a final flourish. When Peggy (who as an adult will turn into an overweight "red hot mama" prostitute) eventually exits her apartment with a basket of laundry, she asks her juvenile suitor what he wants. With a residue of whipped cream on his lips, he awkwardly crunches the empty wrapping paper and stuffs it in his pocket. Completely sated, he sheepishly says, "I'll come back some other time."

Chapter Two

I don't know what my grandfather did for a living, but my father referred to him derisively as a "big shot" (*macher* in Yiddish) in the synagogue, very likely the one right down the street from their tenement building. At one time I had a sepia photograph of him. In the picture I saw a diminutive man dressed, one would assume, in his best suit. His expression was serious, even stern, and his suit jacket proudly displayed a number of unidentifiable medals. There seemed to have been no love lost between my father and my grandfather as the drama played out between the Old World and the New, each attempting to survive in his own way.

When my father was around eleven or twelve years old, he often sat at the kitchen table studying his Hebrew lessons. My grandfather often stood behind my father and, if he recited correctly, my grandfather would occasionally reward him by dropping pennies above his head that would land on the table. My grandfather would tell him, "These are pennies from heaven."

According to my father, who was fast becoming Americanized by this age, this was an Old World custom which he found silly and humiliating.

According to my father, my grandfather had a wicked temper and was given to hitting him "for his own good." One day his father was angry with him for one thing or another—it could have been for something as innocent as playing ball in the street—and, as had happened on previous occasions, he used his belt to reprimand him. In the course of meting out this punishment, common at the time, the metal belt buckle struck my father just above his eye, which resulted in a gash and considerable bleeding. That was the last time my father ever allowed his father to beat him. Soon after that he ran away from home and never returned—either to his home, his Hebrew school, or his public school. At thirteen years of age, my father struck out on his own to make his way in the rough-and-tumble world of the Lower East Side. In doing so he joined the ranks of thousands of street-smart kids who, like him, wanted to free themselves of their punitive, Old-World parents. Al Jolson (born Asa Yoelson) can be counted among them, since he ran away from home (reportedly more than once) beginning at the age of nine, eventually becoming America's most famous and highest paid entertainer, but not necessarily the most loveable or honorable guy in show business. David Sarnoff, another denizen of the Lower East Side, left school at age fifteen to help support his family and make his mark in the world, which he eventually did by becoming a leader in the communications industry, an achievement often accomplished with heartless determination that was not always kosher.

It seems reasonable to assume that Russian and Yiddish were spoken in my father's home. As he grew up, however, he rarely had the opportunity to speak Yiddish since he made his way in a predominantly Christian, *goyisher,* world. Outside the home, at a very young age, he learned to speak English without an accent to avoid being marked as Jewish. Later on, when we lived together in the Bronx, if he wanted to express a bit of Jewish wisdom or humor that didn't translate well to English, he would utter an idiomatic Yiddish phrase and then explain its meaning to me.

By the age of fourteen, boys were legally allowed to apply for working papers and were, ipso facto, considered ready and able to join the labor force. In his meticulously researched book *Made In America*, sociologist Claude S. Fischer points out that "in 1910, about one-half of all fifteen-year-old boys [in the U.S.] were employed." During this era, many so called "documented" teenagers working long hours were only ten years old. By the 1920s and 1930s these abusive child employment practices declined, due to the passage of compulsory education laws and protective child labor laws.

Hester Street was celebrated in the 1975 movie (d: Joan Micklin Silver) of the same name. It tells the story of Yankel Bogovnik, a Russian Jew who emigrates to the United States in 1896 and settles on the eponymous street. Three years later his wife Gitl (superbly played by Carol Kane) arrives with their young son Yossele, only to discover that her husband has assimilated into American life, changed his name to Jake, and has fallen in love with another woman, a dancer named Mamie. The story revolves around Gitl's struggle to adapt to her new world and the decision she eventually has to make as to the kind of life and the kind of husband and father she wants for herself and her son.

Like Gitl, more and more immigrants arrived in America and settled on the Lower East Side. In time the area became increasingly congested. To seek refuge from the overcrowded and often squalid living conditions, many upwardly mobile Jews, Italians, Irish and any number of white Protestant families began moving uptown to Harlem and eventually the Bronx. This migration was made possible by the construction of the city's first regular elevated railway service which began operating in the 1870s running along Greenwich Street and Ninth Avenue. Later on, additional lines ran North and South along Second, Third and Sixth Avenues, thus providing inexpensive transportation originating from Battery Park and South Ferry.

With the arrival of the original elevated rail lines, costing only five-cents to ride, speculators and land developers in Harlem began building row houses, capacious Brownstones, grand mansions and multiple family apartment buildings to house the newcomers. Harlem soon became a churning stewpot of economic and ethnic diversity, with some inhabitants doing quite well, some eking out a living, and some desperately poor. Land developers, hoping to expand their market by appealing to working-class families, began building inexpensive tenements on cheap, odoriferous swamplands . Beginning in 1893 there was a downturn in business and property values dropped precipitously .When the market recovered in 1895 developers built beautiful new apartment buildings. However, in their enthusiasm to turn a quick profit, these developers over-speculated and many houses went unsold and apartments remained un-rented. In order to protect their investments, black landlords decided to fill their empty or partially occupied properties with black tenants. As Harlem became increasingly black, many Jewish families scrambled to better neighborhoods like the Upper West Side, Washington Heights, Central Park West, Brooklyn and the Bronx.

In his well-researched book, *Harlem,* Jonathan Gill reveals that by 1910 there were a hundred thousand Jews living in Harlem. This Jewish population represented the second largest concentration of Eastern European Jews in the country. By the 1920s, he points out, so-called Jewish Harlem, with its many grand synagogues, declined in population from 160,00 in 1923 to 88,000 in 1927 and 25,000 in 1930. By the end of the Great Depression virtually all had left, although some Jews continued to own and operate their retail businesses there. Playwright Arthur Miller was sixteen when the stock market crashed and he and his family were forced to move from their spacious apartment in a fashionable neighborhood of Harlem. George and Ira Gershwin also fled Harlem and rented adjoining penthouses on lower Riverside Drive. Harry Houdini, born Ehrich Weiss in Budapest, Hungary, was the son of a rabbi. At the peak of his popularity as an illusionist and escape artist, he purchased a brand new brownstone house in Harlem around 1904 where he lived until his death in 1926.

According to Gill, Harlem's identity as a black community dates from around 1904 and the coming of the Lenox Avenue IRT subway line, when tens of thousands of black families moved to Harlem looking for work and a better way of life.

With the outbreak of World War I, Harlem once again experienced an influx of black Americans who met the massive demand for unskilled industrial labor to support the war effort. The black newcomers who arrived in Harlem not only found work, but also a haven from the discriminatory Jim Crow laws that prevailed down south. Many of them, along with immigrants from the Caribbean, settled in Harlem as part of the Great Migration, and over time spread out and made the area their own, culturally as well as geographically. Between the years 1918 and the mid-1930s, a black educated class emerged, while top tier writers and musicians gravitated to the area, all of which gave rise to the Harlem Renaissance. The once exclusive residential district in Harlem, as noted above, was eventually abandoned by the white middle and upper-middle classes, who sold their properties to black entrepreneurs and black landlords, who reconfigured many of the stately homes into small apartments and rented them directly to black tenants.

With the expansion of the subway's iron tentacles to the Bronx, it made it possible for residents of the Lower East Side—and those fleeing Harlem—to move to "the country" where they could see the sun rise and set and enjoy fresh air while resting on wooden benches in sprawling leafy parks or on tree-lined boulevards. Jews moving out of Harlem to the Bronx, and directly from the Lower East Side, often expressed their joy with the Yiddish phrase, *khapn a bisl luft* (catching a bit of air).

In the 1920s, spurred by the completion of the Jerome Avenue subway line in 1918, new six-story apartment houses were being built along the Grand Concourse, the final destination for many prosperous Jews, but it also attracted Irish and Italian families along with smatterings of other nationalities all eager to become solid middle-class Americans. In her book *Boulevard of Dreams*, newspaper editor Constance Rosenblum cites the following statistic: "Between 1920 and 1930 the Jewish population in the Bronx doubled, and by the decade's end, the borough was home to 585,000 Jews, the highest concentration in the city." To the best of my knowledge, my mother's family moved from the Lower East Side to the Bronx during this era. Al Jolson sang the praises of the Bronx (ad -libbed with a little too much *schmaltz*) to his mother in *The Jazz Singer* (d: Alan Crosland,1927). "Mama, dahlin, if I'm a success with this show . . . we're going to move up to the Bronx. A whole lot of green grass up there and people you know. The Ginsbergs, the Guttenbergs, the Goldbergs. A whole lot of Bergs. I don't know 'em all."

Chapter Three

Throughout his life, my father depended on his instincts and street smarts to survive. He told me that upon leaving home he found refuge in the basement of a neighborhood bakery where he slept next to the warm ovens during the winter months, earning a few pennies by working for the owner. The details of his life over the next eight or ten years remain sketchy.

In brief conversations over the years, I gleaned that he supported himself, up until the time he married my mother, by working at many different jobs. One was on an assembly line at a watch factory in Connecticut (or upstate New York?) where he painted radium on watch dials to make them glow in the dark. He held this job until he discovered that the metallic element he was working with could be dangerous to your health. Workers ingested poison by repeatedly licking their brush to keep the tip sharp. Later he was one of the first salesmen to introduce the revolutionary Silex Percolator into the marketplace. My father then signed on to sell Van Camps Pork and Beans in the southern part of the United States, a job he held until he was promoted to the position of district manager. I can't be certain of the date, but at some point he decided to leave this job to return to New York.

During his time down south he lodged at a boarding house. One evening he became violently ill and had to be rushed to the local hospital. His appendix had burst and he needed surgery immediately. When he told me this story I was about fourteen, and I remember asking him if he had been scared. He replied in his characteristically terse way, "What's to be scared of. When your time is up, your time is up." That was his philosophy in a nutshell. You lived, you died, and between birth and death you lived your life the best way you could. I believe his life experiences had taught him (as they did me later on) that complaining was pointless. Given his background, it's not surprising that he felt that in this life you're on your own.

The rise of modern salesmanship occurred in the late nineteenth and early twentieth centuries at a time when the world was being transformed by the miracles of science and the spirit of American inventiveness— forces that produced overnight (or so it seemed), the telephone, phonograph, typewriter, electric lights, silent movies, underground subway systems, refrigerated railroad cars to transport meat from Chicago to the nation's eastern cities, and the automobile. And along with all these technological wonders, large manufacturing firms were beginning to turn out an ever-increasing number of new industrial and household products and processed foods to make life a little easier for those who could afford them. Ambitious emigrants, men of all nationalities, with little or no formal education, were hired to introduce and sell these wares from one end of the country to the other. These energetic and adventurous souls, many of them from the Lower East Side, were well suited for the job because, as a general rule, they were unmarried and so were free to travel in pursuit of their Dollar Dreams. My father was one of many foot soldiers enlisted in this new American way of doing business. In his case, his common sense, his keen observation of people—his ability to size them up—and his "get-up-and-go" attitude, proved to be valuable assets in helping him stay afloat in the competitive world of business. Although laconic by nature, he had a storehouse of jokes and stories he would tell to his customers, using a number of different dialects—Irish, Italian, Jewish, southern and "colored." His knack for mimicry and storytelling served him well with his customers and helped get his foot in the door.

In his memoir, *An Hour Before Daylight*, President Jimmy Carter talks about this aspect of salesmanship as it was practiced in Plains, Georgia, where he grew up and worked as a youngster in his Uncle Buddy's retail store, Plains Mercantile Company.

> Despite the competition for sales, there was a sense of camaraderie among the clerks and the many traveling salesmen who served the store. A few of them were serious and all business, but good humor was the normal hallmark of a skilled salesman, and there were almost invariably a few new jokes told during a working day in the store. Some were clean enough to be told to Uncle Buddy and his boys, but others were fit only to share with the men who hung around the barbershop, filling stations, and stable.

This new breed of youthful salesmen saw this calling as an opportunity to escape employment in unsafe New York garment sweatshops, and to learn a skill that would help them climb the ladder of success—which many of them did. By the 1920s the art of salesmanship had been refined and organized, and quickly became a vital cog in the machinery that helped advance consumerism and capitalism to unparalleled heights.

Around 1927, when he met my mother—he was forty-one and my mother was thirty-one—he was selling picture frames with a patented process that laminated a photograph directly into the wood providing permanent protection against fading. One of these picture frames adorned the top of my father's dresser until the day he died. The photograph was a portrait taken (so it would seem) by a professional photographer when my mother was in her late twenties and still very beautiful, before her appearance had been marred by age and her prolonged battle with cancer.

Occasionally, when I was a teenager, I would stand in front of his dresser and stare at my mother's picture hoping to discover something about her that I didn't know. I thought that if I stared into her eyes long enough, they would tell me something about her— some hidden secret about this beautiful young woman I never knew who later became my mother, the woman who carried me in her womb for nine months and then nursed me, fed me, and tenderly rocked me in her arms to comfort me. I wanted to know her dreams and aspirations as a young woman, what she wanted for herself out of life. I also tried to imagine what my father had felt when he first met her, and what he felt whenever he looked at her photograph over the long years after her death.

These experiments of mine were painful and, of course, no revelations were ever forthcoming.

My mother, Florence Sampson, was born in 1896. She emigrated to the United States with her parents from Bialystok (which was part of the Russian empire at the time) and arrived at Ellis Island on November 26, 1901. Bialystok was the largest city in northeastern part of Russia. It had a long history as one of the leading centers of academic, cultural and artistic life in the area. It was also a city of textile mills, department stores and landscaped parks, and was home to a throbbing Zionist movement. During the time my grandparents lived there, the majority of its population was Jewish (including Mel Brooks' mother, Kate Brookman), and anti-Semitism was always in the air. The city was leveled by the Nazis during World War II. (I don't think it was by coincidence that the theatrical producer (played by Zero Mostel), in Mel Brooks' 1967 film, *The Producers*, was named Max Bialystock.)

My mother was five years old when she first set foot on American soil. She arrived with her mother, Ida, and father, Solomon, one older brother, Murray, and two sisters, Frieda and Leah (Lee). The oldest sister, Kate, had arrived by herself earlier. A family photograph of the entire family (minus Kate) was taken about 1905. The three daughters are dressed identically in fashionable Russian-style tunics with matching leather belts and large bow ribbons under their white collars. The children are standing around their parents who are seated in the center. My maternal grandfather, sporting a meticulously trimmed beard, is a thin, handsome man. His facial expression and the fold of his hands suggest warmth and tolerance. My grandmother is wearing a high-necked, long sleeved dress that reaches to the floor. I have only one memory of her from a family gathering at my Uncle Murray's apartment in the Bronx, on University Avenue. I must have been about five at the time, and I noticed her among a crush of relatives. She was standing in a hallway and I remember staring at her. She was the oldest person I had ever seen, and her appearance fascinated me. I don't remember ever speaking to her. She was a stranger to me.

Like my father's family, the Sampsons lived in the densely populated Lower East Side, only a few blocks from where my father's family lived. They settled on Allen Street, a crowded, shadowy street lined with dark and smelly tenement houses, one of them occupied around this time by the German-Jewish parents of lyricist Lorenz "Larry" Hart (of Rodgers and Hart fame). The clatter and rumble of nearby elevated trains sometimes frightened horses below, and dropped cinders and burning coals on pedestrians and housewives, filling the air with soot. Although Allen Street could boast of its own synagogue, it also had to suffer the presence of saloons on nearly every corner and one or more houses of prostitution in the surrounding area.

According to family lore, my aunt Kate was, herself, a prostitute for many years supplementing her work as a hairdresser and manicurist. When I heard this story for the first time I remarked to myself that Aunt Kate literally worked her ass off to save enough money to bring the rest of the family to America. As things worked out, Kate met and married one of her clients, "Uncle" Bob Powell, a nice looking man with a pleasing smile who worked for a circus. My cousin Ruth told me that her mother (my aunt Lee), and my mother, would occasionally hang out with the circus trainers and performers backstage. In the one photograph I have of Bob, he has his arm around Aunt Kate's shoulders. His affection for her appears genuine. Somehow I found out that Uncle Bob was Christian. At the time, I didn't know what to make of this distinction. All I knew was that I liked him. Despite rumors of her past demimonde occupation, and of her marriage to a man outside the Jewish faith, my family seems to have embraced her and "Uncle" Bob. As long as I could remember, they lived together quite happily in an apartment house in the Bronx in the same neighborhood as the rest of my mother's family. While my aunt Kate's somewhat benighted story at this remove of time cannot be verified, I felt it was too good to omit.

If my aunt Kate was, in fact, a prostitute, she had plenty of company in other Jewish women. There has been much written about the fact that wherever Jews put down roots, prostitution sprang up. According to noted scholar Edward J. Bristow in his book *Prostitution and Prejudice: The Jewish Fight Against Slavery*, "By 1889 Jewish women ran 70% of the licensed brothels in eastern Poland and western Russia, an area where Jews were about 12% of the population." He reports that, by 1900 Jewish commercial vice was largely under the control of underworld elements who preyed upon the poor, mostly Jewish women who were earning money in brothels . In many cases, particularly in New York, prostitutes were managed by Jewish men (pimps, who nowadays call themselves "managers" or "agents")—or else they freelanced while keeping house for their husbands, many of whom passed out business cards on the streets to procure customers for their wives. In the late nineteenth and early twentieth centuries, prostitution was one of the few ways for women—especially Jewish women—to earn passage for themselves to America, or to accumulate enough money to send back home to their families. They did this to help their families escape the horrors of pogroms and reach the shores of the United States, where they would have a chance to make a better life for themselves and their children.

Chapter Four

In 1912, when she was sixteen, my mother was quite lovely to look at. In the one picture I have of her at this age she's modishly attired, wearing a white embroidered dress with a scalloped hemline and a pair of high button leather shoes, clearly having adopted American styles. In her left hand she holds her certification of attendance from high school, another sign of assimilation. Slowly but surely, more and more students of all nationalities were enrolling in high school rather than ending their education at the end of the eighth grade, or earlier. By the mid-1920s a good many girls, including those from eastern European Jewish families, had begun attending college(usually Hunter, or in smaller numbers, Barnard).

My cousin Ruth, like my sister, Lucille, is two years older than me. Her mother, Aunt Lee, was my mother's closest sister and best friend and the source of a great deal of information about my mother's life before she met and married my father—information and reminiscences she passed on to Ruth over the years before she had a stroke and died (in 1975 at the age of seventy-three). I remember visiting her in the hospital shortly before her death. The stroke prevented her from speaking, so she scribbled a note on a small white pad and handed it to me. It said, "Help me. I'm trapped in here." I still shudder every time I recall this incident.

According to Aunt Lee, she and my mother would occasionally play tennis and golf at Van Cortland Public Park. Van Cortland, located in the northwestern section of the Bronx, near Woodland cemetery and Mosholu Park, encompasses forty-two acres. The golf course was completed in 1895 and had the distinction of being the first municipal golf course in the nation. In the 1930s other features were added to the park, such as playgrounds, a stadium, parade grounds where soccer games were often played, a bird sanctuary, two nature paths, a cross-country track, a bridle path and a lake for boating.

One day, when I was about four or five, my mother took me with her to the park. My sister was probably in school at the time. Upon our arrival my mother placed me in a supervised play area with a group of other children, while she went off to play tennis or perhaps take a stroll to view the tulips in the Dutch Gardens outside the Van Cortland colonial mansion (an historic home that George Washington reportedly visited on several occasions). I remember being upset with her for leaving me there. I remember, too, walking over to the chain-link fence that enclosed the play area and pressing my face against the cold, diamond-shaped links as I watched my mother slowly walk up a grassy knoll until she disappeared over the crest. At that moment I experienced a sinking feeling as though I might never see her again.

On more than one occasion my mother and Aunt Lee vacationed at Camp Tamiment in the Pocono Mountains in Pennsylvania where they played tennis and other outdoor activities. At this time Jews were not welcome at fashionable summer resorts at Saratoga Springs in the Adirondacks, or in the eastern Long Island coastal towns of Southampton and Bridgehampton. In addition to the few camps available to them in the Poconos, young Jewish women could find refuge from the summer heat in places like the Catskills (otherwise known in those days as the "Jewish Alps" or "Borscht Belt"), or rent a bungalow near the oceanfront in Far Rockaway in Queens, or shuttle down to the Jersey Shore at Atlantic City. They chose the Poconos, which by the 1920s hosted a number of summer camps. One of the most popular among them was Camp Tamiment, which promoted itself as being a place for Jewish singles to meet and enjoy themselves in a high-minded, wholesome atmosphere. Hence tummlers (Yiddish translation: a funmaker, a live wire, a clown, a prankster, the life of the party) were discouraged from showing up. Beginning in 1921,Tamiment provided weeklong vacations in the summer, and the highlight was a Saturday night theatrical revue. This is the same Tamiment where twenty-five years later a young Neil Simon served his apprenticeship writing comedy sketches, and where he met his first wife.

The Catskills resort hotels were so famous in their day, that they often became the source and butt of dozens of jokes. An example: Mrs. Rosenblatt was checking out of her hotel. After she paid her bill, the man behind the front desk asked her, "Did you enjoy your stay?" She replied, "Well, to tell you the truth, the food you serve here is not so great . . . and such small portions!"

My mother, in her pre-marital days, was quite athletic—although not as athletic as my aunt Lee, who was seven years younger. They were the two most Americanized sisters in the family, although according to my cousin Buddy (my mother's brother's son) my mother was the most modern. My aunt Lee recalled that they were both popular with single young men, but that it was my mother, with her good looks and lively personality, whom the men favored. In addition to the fact that my mother was pretty with flowing auburn hair, she also seemed to have good taste. I drew this conclusion after looking at the few pieces of her pottery, glassware and tableware that my sister and I have held onto. She also must have had an inquisitive mind, because I can remember my father telling me that she and Aunt Lee would frequently attend evening lectures in the neighborhood on a variety of topics. Attending lectures was fashionable in those days for young men and women with an intellectual bent. It was an educational activity that could be traced to the Lower East Side at the turn of the century, when poor, overworked immigrants flocked to them on Friday and Saturday nights in search of an experience to expand their education. My father—who was already forty-nine by 1935—told me he was content to stay home most evenings, reading the newspaper as well as pulp fiction stories about the American frontier by Zane Grey and Max Brand, while taking care of my sister and I so that my mother could continue her practice of going out to lectures.

In addition to my mother's intellectual curiosity, vivacity, and athletic interests (which she enjoyed when she wasn't suffering with blinding headaches) she was also musical. A Steinway baby grand piano occupied a place of pride in our living room.

My sister, in one of her rare childhood memories, recalls our mother playing two of Beethoven's romantic pieces, " Für Elise" and the "Moonlight Sonata." My sister also recalls our mother teaching her to play the piano and taking her on a long trolley ride once a week to Mt. Vernon for private lessons in someone's home. In many Jewish homes in the early years of the 20th century learning to play the piano—for families that could afford the cost of fifty cents a lesson—was considered part of a child's education on the road to Americanization. I can only assume that when my mother was growing up, her parents could afford this musical luxury.

I don't have any detailed memories of my mother playing the piano, but I do remember her drawing on a large white artist's pad with pastel chalks of many colors and shades which she kept neatly stored in separate compartments in a wooden box with a gold-colored latch. She also had a lovely voice. I can clearly remember playing with my Lincoln Logs on the living room floor and listening to her sing in the kitchen, while she baked Linzer Tarts with dollops of raspberry in the center. During this period of my life, I slept in a crib in my parents' bedroom. My sister, as I remember, slept on a folding cot at the foot of my parent's bed. These were the years when my mother was in and out of the hospital, undergoing several different surgeries to save her from the cancer which eventually claimed her life in 1939—after only eleven years of marriage.

My mother married my father in September, 1928 when she was thirty-two years old. My father was forty-two. After so many rootless years, I think my father wanted to settle down, and when he met my mother something inside of him must have said, "This is the woman for me," or "This is the woman I've been waiting for," or something like that. I imagine that my mother felt she could be happy with my father living in the Bronx near her parents and her large extended family consisting of her four siblings, and assorted cousins, nieces and nephews . . . and no potentially intrusive in-laws to contend with. My father had two sisters, Lena and Rose, but he was not very close to them. They lived in Brooklyn. For my father, a man of few needs, I believe the love and affection of a wife and children were all he needed to be happy. It's entirely conceivable that, when he met my mother, he saw this as his chance to fulfill his dream of having a family of his own—a wholesome, loving family, unlike the one he had fled as a youth.

The cultural climate in the country during the time my parents found each other was succinctly described by historian Arthur M. Schlesinger, Jr., in his memoir, *A Life In The 20th Century.* He categorized this period as "an era of contradictions—the decade at once of fundamentalism and flappers, prohibitionists and bootleggers, a book on Main Street and a boom on Wall Street, disenchantment with war and enchantment with business." Along with drastic changes in beliefs and customs that swept the country, women's fashions also changed, and I have a feeling, that my mother and Aunt Lee tried to keep up with the latest trends. Gone were the ankle-length skirts and dresses and whalebone corsets of an earlier time. Beginning in 1923 hemlines began to rise so that by 1927 they reached the knee and even above—much to the delight, I'm sure, of the male population. However, not all men were pleased with these new fashion trends. In Utah, the state legislature considered sending women to prison—not just fining them—if their skirts showed more than three inches of leg above the ankle.

At about the same time the waistline had moved to the hips, giving women a slimmer, more boyish outline. In general, women's clothes, and underwear, were redesigned to give flappers, newly emancipated women, the freedom to dance the Charleston, the Shimmy, the Bunny Hug, or the more scandalous Black Bottom (which involved hopping forward and backward and slapping the rump), all dances which became popular during the Jazz Age. Black, white and brown stockings were replaced by flesh-colored ones, made of silk or the new, less expensive man-made fibre, rayon. Long hair, as a fashion, was also disappearing. By 1926, two years before my mother married, most "girls"(as young women were called at the time) were wearing their hair short, or "bobbed"—which is to say cut short and even all the way around. This and other changes in hair styles ushered in the permanent wave, giving a boost to the beauty parlor business where women flocked in hopes of achieving "It," (epitomized in those days by silent screen star Clara Bow) or "sex appeal," a new term that reportedly came into vogue during the Roaring Twenties.

By 1933, the year I was born (also the year that Prohibition officially ended) the flat-chested, long-waisted flapper look had begun to disappear and women's waistlines and bustline were back where nature intended them to be. Regarding their upper torso, some women even tried, as one writer quipped, "to make mountains out of molehills." At the same time skirt lengths dropped to at least midcalf. By the late 1920s, or early 1930s, the slouch—a soft felt hat with a high crown and drooping brim, usually pulled down over one eye, Greta Garbo-style—replaced the bell-shaped clouche as the most popular women's hat.

I suspect by this time, and certainly by 1937,my mother didn't have the time, money, or the energy to care about which direction women's waists or bustlines were moving, or what women were wearing on their heads. My mother had aged considerably by then. In the brownish photograph I have of her at age 40—taken on the beach at Sea Gate, Brooklyn, where my Aunt Lee and her family lived at the time—my mother is wearing white shorts and a shirt. Her hair is short and wavy. She is seated on the sand with her arms wrapped around my sister and I, staring blankly into the camera. I have no way of knowing what she was thinking or feeling at this time, approximately three years before she died. Every time I look at this picture a deep sadness stirs within me over what could have been for her and all of us had she lived.

Chapter Five

Movies were all the rage in the 1920s, and I'm sure my parents (probably my mother more than my father) were regular moviegoers—along with about fifty-seven million other people who attended the movies on a weekly basis by 1927. Like the others, my parents more than likely had their favorite "bigger-than-life" silent screen movie stars. By the beginning of the decade, when movies were fast becoming the most popular form of mass entertainment in the country, there were approximately 16,000 movie houses. An increasing number of them (especially in New York) were opulent "dream" palaces built as early as 1914, some with a seating capacity up to 2,500. Loew's Paradise, located on the Grand Concourse south of Fordham Road, was the showplace movie theater of the Bronx, and one of the last "atmospheric" neighborhood theaters erected in the United States. Built in 1929 at a cost of four million dollars, the ornate interior, with red velour seats, was designed to resemble an Italian baroque garden with stars twinkling high above in a cavernous night sky and filmy clouds drifting over the dark blue heavens. With a capacity of approximately four thousand seats, it was second in size in New York only to the Roxy Theater, built near Times Square in 1927 with nearly six-thousand seats, and to Radio City Musical Hall, also with six-thousand seats. The Paradise attracted many working- and middle-class families, as well as teenagers with their Saturday night dates, many of whom, I'm sure, experienced their first kiss in the balcony. Who knows, maybe my parents went there to attend the Grand Opening, exactly one month to the year after they were married. It wasn't that far from where they lived on Andrews Avenue, and it would have been a swell way—and within their economic means—for them to celebrate their first wedding anniversary.

Radio City Music Hall, located on 50th Street near 6th Avenue, opened its doors on December 27, 1932. My father took my sister and I there during the 1940s. I remember sitting in the orchestra at intermission listening to the thunderous sound of the "Mighty Wurlitzer" pipe organ performed live under a bright spotlight. While the music resonated throughout the theater, members of the audience watched the screen as a bouncing ball kept tune with the music and highlighted the words to the song, "In My Merry Oldsmobile," so we could all sing along. It was a wondrous moment of camaraderie and peacefulness; you felt you were part of a mass of humanity gently floating down a lazy river with thousands of people lined up along the shore singing joyously. It was as close as I ever got— with my croaky voice and tin ear—to singing with a chorus.

I'd like to believe my parents, before they knew each other, had the time and money to see the comic genius of Harold Lloyd in *Safety Last* (d: Neymeyer and Taylor, 1923), and Charlie Chaplin in *The Gold Rush* (d: Chaplin, 1925) . . . and maybe, after they met, to see Al Jolson in *The Jazz Singer*— the first motion picture to incorporate singing and a few lines of dialogue into a silent feature-length film (hence the first "talkie"). It premiered October 23, 1927 at the Warner Bros. flagship Strand Theater in Times Square. If my father did go see this movie, I wonder how he reacted when he watched a young Jakie Rabinowitz (later "Jack Robin" played by Al Jolson) about to be whipped with a belt by his stern, religious father. In the film the boy looks defiantly at his father and the title card on the screen reads, "If you whip me again, I'll run away . . . I'll never come back." After the beating Jakie leaves his Lower East Side apartment, but returns later to retrieve a photograph of his mother who, in a later scene, is seen weeping in a tight close-up. Her rueful words are spelled out on the inter-title: "Our boy is gone and he is never coming back." Maybe seeing this film together, if, indeed they did, made it possible for my father to open up to my mother about his unhappy childhood.

On another occasion, maybe when my father had some extra money in his pocket from a bonus or a salary increase, he decided to show my mother "a swell time" by taking her to see the Broadway musical *Show Boat* which opened on December 27, 1927 at the Ziegfeld Theater. Or, after they were married, maybe they got to see the movie *The Broadway Melody* (d: Harry Beaumont, 1929), released by MGM. It was a backstage musical and the first sound film to win an Academy Award for Best Picture. At any rate, these were the times they lived in and I like to imagine them enjoying some of these popular cultural attractions during their courtship and honeymoon days.

During the 1920s, eating out was almost as popular a form of entertainment as going to the movies. This decade marked the birth of the modern restaurant industry: after prohibition stripped away liquor profits from high-end restaurants, thousands of low-priced, high-volume restaurants opened their doors—staffed, for the first time in many locations, by female servers. The industry's motto was "clean and fast" service to cater to businessmen, assembly-line workers, department store clerks and secretaries on their way to work in the morning or during their lunch break. The biggest change during the twenties was that restaurants were no longer places where you went just to eat. Many of them became places to socialize, to gossip, to make business deals, to have a few drinks (under the table), to dance and listen to jazz or popular music. In small towns and large cities, people from all walks of life, frequented the growing number of restaurants, from fancy hotel dining rooms to elegant independently-owned restaurants. In New York, these included Luchow's near Union Square, New York's quintessential German restaurant, established in 1882; Delmonico's fine French restaurant in lower Manhattan, the progenitor of a fine dining restaurant culture in America, which closed its doors in 1923 after almost one hundred years in service; and the Russian Tea Room on West 57th, home to celebrities, which was opened in 1926 by exiled members of the Russian Imperial Ballet who fled the Bolshevik Revolution. More moderately priced diners, cafeterias, luncheonettes, coffee shops, automats, drive-ins, ethnic restaurants featuring Italian and Chinese dishes, and chain restaurants with their own individual architectural styles, opened for business at this time.

In addition, tens of thousands of roadside eateries sprang up across the country, catering to motorists, sightseers, traveling salesmen and vacationers. This growing segment of the food-service industry was bolstered considerably by the fact that the number of automobiles on the road jumped from 8 million in 1920 to 23 million in 1930. Since my father was on the road six days a week, I'm sure he frequented his share of diners, his favorite stopping-off place for breakfast and lunch. I, too, enjoyed eating at diners, especially on Saturdays since my father didn't return home from work until around two in the afternoon. There was one such diner a half block from our apartment house where I either ordered a hamburger or, if I was extra hungry, the blue plate special.

I have so many unanswered questions about my parents' lives before and after they met. I have often wondered if either of them were part of the crush of humanity standing on the sidewalks up and down Fifth Avenue on November 21, 1918 (when my mother was twenty-two years old), watching the passing parade of soldiers and marines marching under a shower of ticker-tape to celebrate the Armistice which officially ended World War I. Eight years later, on August 23, 1926, did my mother and Aunt Lee crane their necks—along with 10,000 other female fans—in the sweltering heat along West 66th Street to get a view of the casket carrying the body of Rudolph Valentino? Five years before his death Valentino starred in *The Sheik* (d: George Melford, 1921), the movie that catapulted him into stardom and made him the world's undisputed "Great Lover" of the silent screen. I wonder if my mother went to see him in this film, when she was twenty-five years old. I also wonder if my mother and father had known each other on May 22, 1927 (about sixteen months before they were married), when the morning newspapers screamed the news that Charles Lindbergh had raced across the Atlantic Ocean on a non-stop solo flight from New York to Paris in just thirty-three and half hours. Did they attend, along with millions of other well-wishers, the ticker-tape parade up Broadway on June 13—reportedly the wildest reception in the city's history—to watch Mayor Jimmy Walker pin New York's Medal of Valor on Lindbergh's chest? In the 1920s it was not uncommon for people to gather in enormous numbers for almost any event.

There is no argument that Charles Lindbergh was the most skilled aviator of his day. When he was up in the clouds he was rarely lost. On the ground, however, his moral and intellectual compass failed him miserably. Over time his reputation was tarnished by his naiveté and narrow-mindedness which caused him to fly repeatedly into storms of controversy. By all accounts he was a Nazi sympathizer who believed Adolf Hitler was a "great man." Lindbergh was an anti-Semite who blamed the Jews (along with Britain and FDR) for agitating for war against Germany during the 1930s. He was a proponent of the crackpot science of eugenics, and an isolationist up until the day Japan bombed Pearl Harbor. In a biography published in 2005 it was revealed that Lindbergh, the wholesome family man, had had clandestine love affairs with several women in postwar Germany producing a number of children. After the sneak attack on Pearl Harbor Lindbergh polished up his reputation by offering his services to a number of aviation companies and eventually took part in flying combat raids on Japanese installations.

As I imagine my parents' lives and the era in which they lived, I can only hope they found time to enjoy their marriage—before the Great Depression began in 1929, before my sister was born in 1930, before I was born in 1933, and before my mother became too ill, too soon, to find enjoyment in much of anything. It's interesting to note that my parents decided to have children at a time when most people were postponing this decision, which is borne out by the fact that the birthrate during the Depression was the lowest in U.S. history. Perhaps they felt that, at their age, they didn't have the luxury of time.

Like me, James "Scotty" Reston (of *New York Times* fame) said he wished he had known more about his mother's early life, even though she lived to be ninety eight. Despite the fact that he was a newspaper reporter all his life, and therefore used to asking people questions, he never got around to quizzing his own mother. In his memoir, *Deadline,* he wrote: "We often wonder about the early lives of our own parents, for it's hard for us to imagine them when they were young and full of the love that brought us into the world. We usually think of them when they were in middle age, caught between their own rebellious children and their aging parents, or when they were too old to remember." Unfortunately for me, by the time I began to wonder about my parents' early lives, they were no longer around for me to ask. But that doesn't stop me from wondering if, like most people, when they first met and married, they shared their hopes and dreams—maybe over a restaurant dinner, or in bed before drifting off to sleep - of a bright future together. Perhaps they were content merely to have met each other; maybe that alone was enough for them without wishing for more, especially during the Great Depression. At the time, maybe the best they could hope for, at least in the near future, was to be able to afford to rent a two-bedroom apartment which would have been a luxury for them. Knowing my father, I'm confident he had aspirations before he met my mother of making something more of himself; of finding some way to achieve financial success.

In the 1920s many men must have shared my father's aspirations, and why not? During this decade, America became the wealthiest country in the world. According to Bill Bryson's detailed account of 1927, in his book *One Summer*, "Inflation was zero and had been for four years. Economic growth was averaging 3.3 percent a year. The latest figures from the Treasury Department . . . showed that for the fiscal year just completed the United States had enjoyed a record budget surplus of $630 million and had trimmed $1 billion off the national debt." Bankers, stockbrokers, industry leaders and ordinary citizens believed that prosperity was here to stay. Jobs were plentiful (especially in big city factories) and people had a lot of spare cash to spend. And with the introduction of installment payments, people got in the habit of getting what they wanted now and not worrying too much about paying for it later. This was the circular flow of money expressed by John Maynard Keynes. It was his economic theory (in part) that if people (the working- and middle-class people) were spending money to purchase consumer goods and services—electric refrigerators, vacuum cleaners, ready-to-wear clothes, automobiles and radios—then people had to be employed to make the things people wanted, and the cycle (helped by increased government spending during sluggish periods) would continue on and on. I can imagine that, for my parents, it must have seemed like a propitious time to get married and start a family.

For a few people eager to get rich fast, this sense of optimism and enthusiasm gave birth to any number of clever, and not so clever, Get-Rich-Quick schemes. Emblematic of the times was Italian immigrant Charles Ponzi, a charismatic rogue who launched the most famous scam in the history of American finance and whose name today is synonymous with any "rob Peter to pay Paul" financial scheme. His grand enterprise lasted approximately eight months before he was charged, convicted, and sent to a federal prison for three and a half years. The most recent scoundrel to employ Ponzi's tactics is Bernie Madoff, currently behind bars.

In his book *Ponzi's Scheme*, author Mitchell Zuckoff describes the mood of the country in the decade before the 1929 Wall Street collapse destroyed the lives and dreams of millions of Americans. It was a time, he wrote, when anything seemed possible, especially when it came to amassing money:

> A new ethos was emerging, one that would reshape what it meant to be an American. No more pennies saved and pennies earned. Money was best when it arrived fast, easy, and in large quantities. Newspapers fueled the dreams of prosperity with stories of poor girls marrying rich men, inherited fortunes from long-lost relatives, and fearless entrepreneurs who'd hit it big. The message was clear: No longer was prosperity the preserve of the well-born; even the laborer and the charwoman could aspire to the

manor. All it took was the right break, the right knocks at the door.

In America, at the turn of the century and for decades beyond, there was something in the air that captured the imagination of men of all age, men who were determined to capitalize on America's financial success. One way to accomplish this (legally) was to invent something. It was like a flu epidemic that spread across the land infecting thousands of men, some of them with only an eighth grade education, who were convinced this was the quickest path forward to big money. They would go to work during the day, and at night and on weekends, in their garages, basements, backyards or kitchens, they would tinker with pieces of wood, leather, cotton fabric, metal, or electrical wiring until they had created something the world could use. During this period the spirit of creativity sparked a diverse number of inventions: thumbtacks (1900), the first "pop-up" toaster (1919), Band-Aids (1920), masking tape (1921), ice cube trays (1928), electric razors (1928), and staple removers (1932)— to name just a few of the products and gadgets that were introduced into the marketplace. Dedicated inventors looked up to men like Thomas Alva Edison who was credited with inventing the first incandescent light bulb, the phonograph and motion pictures (and in his spare time, inventing reasons to dislike Jews); Isaac Singer who invented the Singer Sewing machine; Henry Ford (a friend of Edison and rabid Anti-semite) who introduced the first readily affordable mass produced automobile, the "Model T" (a.k.a. "Tin Lizzy"); George Eastman, who developed the first Kodak camera and roll film for still and motion picture cameras;

Guglielmo Marconi who developed the first effective system for radio communication; Alexander Graham Bell, who engineered the first practical telephone; Orville and Wilbur Wright who were noted for their contribution to aviation; and Gustavus Franklin Swift, who invented the first ice-cooled railroad car to ship dressed meats across the country. My father, like thousands of other men of his generation, was bitten by the invention bug; it made him believe there was nothing he couldn't do if he put his mind to it.

In his spare time, before and after my mother's death, my father devised several inventions. Unfortunately, none of them bore fruit. They did succeed, however, in keeping him busy and keeping his dream alive that one day he, too, would strike it rich. One of these inventions was a full-length brown plastic garment that snapped on over the front of a worker's clothes; it was meant to prevent any part of his clothing from getting sucked into the machinery he was working on. Instead of a sleeve or the front of a shirt getting entangled in the machinery (especially by conveyor belts in assembly-line manufacturing plants), the garment my father devised would get caught and immediately "snap off" the worker, preventing him from serious injury. At this time there was little concern for worker safety, and accidents were the worker's problem, not the company's. Another invention my father came up with was a comb cleaner. It looked and worked like the leather strop used for sharpening straight razors (still used at the beginning of the twentieth century). Instead of leather, my father's invention used multicolored strands of cotton thread. The user would hook one end of the cleaner to a faucet or doorknob. With one hand he would hold the cleaner taut and with the other hand he would run the comb back and forth through the strips of thread to release the lint caught between the teeth of the comb. When the comb cleaner got dirty, the user simply rinsed it in soap and hot water and it was ready to use again. Another invention that he was still working on in the 1940s, was a small metal clamp that would fit over the stem sticking out from the rubber tube incased inside a tire. My father's handy little device, which a man could carry around in his pocket, prevented the tube's stem from slipping beneath the hole in the metal rim when you pressed the head of the air hose down to inflate the tube with air. By the mid-1950s tubeless tires began to appear in the marketplace nullifying the need for my father's invention.

In looking back on this part of his life, it seems to me that these inventions say something about my father's nature, in that each one of them was designed to make people's lives either easier or safer. On another level, even though he was most likely unaware of it, his inventions adhered to the basic marketing principle: *find a hole and fill it.* Unfortunately, my father was one of the unlucky tinkerers who never made it, but he was still at it well into his sixties.

Chapter Six

In 1996, during a visit to Connecticut, I asked my Cousin Buddy, who is ten years my senior, why my father was treated as an outsider by my mother's family. He said it was because my father was "goyisher," translated as having "Gentile brains" or "Gentile ways," in either case a pejorative Yiddish expression that inferred that his mannerisms and his way of thinking made him different (un-Jewish, if you will); not one of the tribe. Unlike my mother's sisters and brother, my father had no family he could fall back on; no family to turn to for assistance or comfort, and virtually no familiarity with family gatherings and the pleasantry of social chit chat. For most of his life he had been on his own, a loner, unaccustomed to the conviviality and intermingling that are a feature of family life. From a very young age he had been part of the world of commerce, dominated by non-Jews; a world which helped shape his "goyisher" mannerisms and views. I think he must have found it difficult to make small talk, to *kibbitz* or *schmooze*, with my mother's family. It must have seemed foreign to him, thus leaving the impression he was anti-social and standoffish.

As a child and as an adult, my father never had the experience described by Russell Baker in his captivating Depression-era memoir, *Growing Up.* As a young boy, Baker, out of financial necessity, lived in New Jersey with his mother, his young sister, his aunt and uncle, and two unemployed uncles. Lying in bed at night he would listen to his family gabbing around the kitchen table with a pot of coffee on the stove:

> Besides politics they talked about movies, philosophy, and morals. Methods for banking a coal furnace. How to outwit the electric company by putting in meter "cheaters." About their high-school Latin teacher, Professor Brent, who'd known Woodrow Wilson . . . About the rotten deal Herbert Hoover had given the boys who fought in France. They debated the relative merits of crooners—Bing Crosby v. Rudy Vallee . . . Argued about baseball. Joked about Roosevelt's "brain trust." Reminisced about the time ancient Aunt Henrietta was mistaken for a ghost by two carpenters and scared them so badly they jumped out the second floor window.

Like so many men in his line of work, my father was used to impersonal hotels and boarding houses and restaurant food. He was used to a solitary, self-sufficient life on the road, and he grew accustomed to this insulated way of living for so long that I think it was almost impossible for him to mingle casually with family members. From what I observed of him over the years, I don't think he knew how to relax, how to let himself go and have fun with other people. There is no denying he was a "loner," a quality that had crystallized in him long before he met and married my mother.

Having said this, I don't think he lived his life entirely alone. Over the years, as I got to know him better, especially when we were living together when I was in college, I sensed the presence of a constant "inner companion" with whom he shared his life. It was as though he were married to a certain set of principles that guided his thoughts and actions, and that allowed him to measure himself in a way that gave meaning to his life. As rewarding as this interior relationship might have been, it is sad that he lived most of his life without the comfort and warmth of a woman. For my part I tried as much as I could—as much as a kid can—to make him feel needed and loved.

My father's alienation from my mother's family—before and after her death—was palpable, but not overt. I always had the feeling, even as a kid, that there was an unspoken conspiracy against him that manifested itself through attitude and body language, and by the fact that no member of my mother's family made an effort (that I can recall) to reach out to him, or to stay in touch with him after my mother's death. The exception was Aunt Lee who, as far as I remember, never said anything disrespectful about my father—except for the time she lost her temper and threw a pot at his head (more later about that). It may be, too, that my mother's family's cool treatment of my father had to do with his pride or stubbornness—his go-it-alone-mentality—which made it difficult for him to ask for help or place his burdens on someone else's shoulders. This reminds me of the following story:

An elderly Jew carrying a heavy bundle was walking along a dusty, country road on a hot summer's day in Poland at the turn of the twentieth century. As luck would have it, a man in a horse-driven cart came along and offered him a ride. The Jew graciously accepted. He got up on the seat next to the man but he kept his heavy bundle on his lap. The man said to him, why don't you put the bundle down on the floor board and rest a little. That's okay, the Jew said, I'm used to carrying it around, and besides, why should I give the poor horse something else to carry. (In this story, as originally told, maybe the bundle he was "used to carrying around" was the symbolic burden of anti-Semitism that he could never put down, but it can also be interpreted , for our purposes, as the heavy load of responsibility that rested on my father's shoulders year after year.)

By nature, my father was abstemious and extremely honest, and he always voted the Democratic ticket. He was not a tall man. He probably topped out at five foot four in adulthood, a trait I inherited that made my teenage years more challenging than they otherwise had to be. After he married he managed to stay in shape because of the physical labor he performed every day, tossing automobile tires on and off his truck. Even as he got older and put on a little weight around his midsection, he was never seriously overweight and was always nimble on his feet. At some point, before or after he got married, he developed a hernia on the right side of his abdomen. He told me he never had the money to pay for an operation so he lived with a slab of flesh, resembling an elderly woman's sagging breast, that protruded from his abdomen. In lieu of an operation doctors advised him to wear a belted corset around his stomach for support, an apparatus he faithfully strapped on every morning to avoid further injury. He also had a scar on his right calf which, if I remember correctly, had something to do with the threat of gangrene, which I never fully understood, but because of the seriousness of this condition he was forced to quit smoking. At some stage in his life he began wearing glasses, yet for as long as we lived together I can never remember him going for an eye exam or getting a new pair.

Given that my mother was one of the more Americanized members of her family, it could well have been my father's non-Jewish ways that appealed to her. But my cousin Ruth offered another possibility. According to her mother, my mother decided to marry my father, in part, because she felt she could trust him. Perhaps she saw in him someone she could count on for understanding and comfort when she suffered one of the excruciating headaches that could disable her for days or weeks at a time. Despite her valiant efforts to be outgoing, she probably was in frail health from time to time when they met, and may have sensed a steadiness—his bedrock-like constitution - that she could lean on in the future. I'm sure she also thought he would make a good father, something most women (then and now) consider carefully before marrying. When I asked my father how they met, he replied, in his usual taciturn fashion, that they met at a party at a friend's house. It seems that my mother mentioned to him that her radio was not working and he offered to come over and repair it. That's all he told me. But again, unfortunately, it didn't occur to me to ask him for more details.

Assuming my parents knew each other in 1927, a little over a year before they married, I can believe how eager my mother must have been to have her radio repaired. For her, and millions like her, radio had become the technological wonder of the age. It got its start when the first commercial radio station (KDKA) in Pittsburgh began broadcasting in 1920. Three years later there were more than 500 stations across the country filling the airwaves with low-cost, unimaginative programming, mostly local speeches. It wasn't long before music found a home on radio. In 1922 the Boston Symphony Orchestra broadcast the first live radio concert. Not too long after, classical music gave way to popular singers, like crooners Bing Crosby and Rudy Vallee, and dance bands like Paul Whiteman's Orchestra. Before paid advertising became an acceptable business practice, many orchestras—in order to boost name recognition for the companies footing the bills—were named for the sponsor, like the Ipana (toothpaste) Troubadours, the A&P (grocery chain) Gypsies, the Cliquot Club (soda water) Eskimos, and so on.

In 1925 more than 70 percent of air time was given over to music. This trend was soon followed by another—comedy shows. One of the first of its kind, and soon to be one of the most popular radio program on the air, was "Amos 'n' Andy" which premiered over station WMAQ in Chicago in 1928 under the sponsorship of Pepsodent toothpaste. I can just imagine my mother and father sitting around the radio in their one-bedroom apartment listening in companionable silence (as most people did), interrupted occasionally by brief outbursts of laughter. As a testament to radio's popularity, the May, 1922 issue of *The Saturday Evening Post* devoted its front cover to a

Norman Rockwell illustration entitled "Old Couple Listening to Radio"—one of his most memorable images of small-town American life.

That year about 400,000 radio sets (mostly listened to with headsets) were in use in the United States; by 1928 the number had increased more than twenty-fold to 8.5 million; and by 1932 that number had increased to 18 million. With all the wonderful entertainment streaming into people's homes, it wasn't long before radio replaced reading as the nation's principal in-home pastime.

In the 1920s, before radio became a permanent fixture in people's homes, American publishers, according to Bryson, "produced 110 million books, more than 10,000 separate titles, double the number of ten years before". . . and gave birth to a new literary phenomenon, the Book-of-the Month Club followed by the Literary Guild. New magazines also began appearing on the nation's newsstands, including *Reader's Digest, Time, American Mercury* and *The New Yorker*, as well as a number of cheap tabloid newspapers with their screaming headlines. But radio had something special to offer. It brought "live" music, comedy, drama, sports, local and national news and major cultural events into people's homes. On November 2, 1920, the night Warren G. Harding defeated Democrat James Cox to become President of the United States , radio was used for the first time to broadcast coverage of the election results and it was heard by maybe a thousand people wearing earphones. It also marked the first election in which women could vote, a political victory I'm certain my mother and Aunt Lee celebrated.

Perhaps less important but equally compelling was the use

of radio, along with the press, to provide coverage of the sensational Leopold and Loeb case in 1925 in which two extremely wealthy college students kidnapped and murdered a fourteen-year-old boy for "the thrill of it." That same year radio listeners could hear live coverage (from microphones set up inside the courtroom) of another famous trial, in which science teacher John Scopes was accused of teaching evolution in public schools in the state of Tennessee. Dubbed the "Scopes Monkey Trial," it was the first live radio broadcast of a trial in American history. Two years later, on June 11, 1927, people could tune in their radios to hear the live remarks President Calvin Coolidge made to Charles Lindbergh on his triumphal return home from Paris. On August 22 of the same year, two Italian emigrants (and anarchists of sorts), Sacco and Vanzetti, were sent to the electric chair after being convicted of the murder of two men in a payroll heist in South Braintree, MA. The local radio stations in the Boston area announced that they would remain on the air past their usual ten o'clock sign-off time to bring their listeners news of the midnight executions. Also broadcast in 1927 was the first World Series between the Yankees and the Giants. Most people at this time considered it magical, if not a miracle, to hear a live human voice emanate from a box sitting inside their home, or in the case of gangster Al Capone(America's Public Enemy Number One), in his cell in an Atlanta prison where he and his chummy guards would listen to their favorite shows during the 1930s.

With the advent of radio advertising, and the colossal revenue it generated (largely at the expense of daily newspapers), radio stations multiplied, and with the help of new technology it was possible, for the first time in history, for people all across the nation to hear the same live event at the same time. The National Broadcasting Company (NBC) pioneered this advancement in 1927 when it inaugurated the country's first radio network with coast-to-coast hookups. Two years later millions of people listening to their radios at home heard the inauguration of President Hoover on 120 stations broadcasting across the country. Never before had a consumer product been so widely accepted and wildly embraced in so short a period of time. It was doubtful that a single person in the country, my mother included, would have wanted to miss out on all the excitement and pleasures radio had to offer.

Chapter Seven

On Thursday, October 24, 1929—approximately one year after my parents married—Wall Street collapsed and the Great Depression began. Within the first thirty days $30 billion worth of stock value vanished into thin air. As reported at the time, about 80,000 businesses went to the wall, 5,000 banks failed, some 60,000 farmers lost their land to foreclosure, and the national income was cut in half. Capitalism, to the glee of some and the sorrow of others, had apparently exhausted itself in a downward spiral and there was no one to answer for it. There was just an echoing silence, interrupted by the occasional thud of a body hitting the pavement after plummeting from an office window high above the city.

By December, 1932, two years after my sister was born, nearly one of every four employable New Yorkers was jobless. By March, 1933,unemployment peaked at 15 million, and on Wednesday, March 4, three days after I was born, Franklin D. Roosevelt was inaugurated as the 32nd president of the United

States. One of the first things he did to prevent more banks from failing, was to declare a "Bank Holiday," which meant that for approximately one week my parents couldn't cash a paycheck or withdraw money from their savings account. As if this financial hardship weren't enough, on the other side of the world, political events were shaping up in Europe that would eventually lead to the start of World War II. This was not an auspicious beginning for my parents' marriage, and it only got worse.

As a result of the financial crash, many families lost their homes to bank foreclosures. In large cities mothers and their children were found huddled together in apartments near starvation while their husbands were out scavenging for food. Breadlines became a common sight, and homeless people found refuge under bridges, in railroad cars, in missions and municipal shelters. Thousands lined up at the Salvation Army or the Red Cross to get a simple meal. Somehow my father managed to survive this financial catastrophe, as I don't remember ever missing a meal or going to bed hungry. Be that as it may, I'd have to believe that my parents, like most everyone else, lived in constant fear that they too might go under, as happened to my aunt Lee when her husband, Leon, found himself unemployed and no longer able to pay the rent. His older sister, Anna, who owned a large home in Bensonhurst, Brooklyn, offered to take them in. The three of them—my aunt Lee, my uncle Leon, and my cousin Ruth, who was about three or four at the time—occupied a small room (at no cost until my uncle could get back on his feet) in the rear of her house.

I don't know what my father did for a living the first few years he was married to my mother. But by the mid-thirties he had managed to work out an arrangement that made it possible for him to go into business for himself on a modest scale. The deal my father hashed out was with Jaffe Tire Company on Jerome Avenue in the Bronx, not far from where we lived. Mr. Jaffe, who had started the company in the early 1930s, was in the business of recapping tires which proved much cheaper than buying new ones. Even new ones, during this era, were not made to last long. They were made up of a thin rubber balloon inside a hard circle of rubber that wrapped around a steel rim. A board with nails or a piece of glass in the road were like daggers at the throat of these poorly made tires. Business picked up considerably with the outbreak of World War II when very few if any new tires were being produced for the civilian population—especially after Japan invaded Malaya in 1942 and cornered most of the world's rubber supply. Mr. Jaffe assigned the entire county of Westchester to my father as his sales territory, which meant that he was pretty much in business for himself. To help my father get started, Mr. Jaffe leased a brand new Chevrolet van for my father to travel around in. My father would visit virtually every gas station and auto repair shop in the county to pick up balding tires to be recapped back at the plant. After this process he would return them to their original location. He earned his money by marking up the price Jaffe charged to include a profit for himself for the pick-up and delivery service he provided.

On any given day my father would drive between fifty and seventy-five miles, six days a week (half day on Saturday) picking up and delivering tires. To avoid any mix-ups my father marked the sidewall of each tire with a bright yellow crayon bearing the customer's name and the location where the tire was picked up. My father was still picking up and delivering tires until the day he died.

It could not have been easy for my parents during these precarious times: they were living in a one-bedroom apartment with two small children while my mother battled cancer, my mother's aging and ailing mother living downstairs in an apartment with my aunt Lee, and my sister requiring two separate mastoid operations behind her right ear to save her from going deaf. (Today mastoids would be successfully treated with antibiotics.) One way or the other, my father saw to it that his family survived these dark days. All of this must have dampened the happiness that all married couples have a right to expect in the early years of their marriage—especially newlyweds who had waited so long to find each other.

My father told me he first became aware that something was not quite right with my mother when, one night, he and my mother were coming home from grocery shopping. They were in the elevator on the way up to our apartment and my mother was talking about what she was going to prepare for dinner, when suddenly she switched to an entirely different subject. After this curious incident my father made an appointment with a doctor to have her examined. I can only imagine how frightened she must have been at the prospect of undergoing a neurological exam and fearing the worst from it. Knowing my father, I'm sure he comforted her every step of the way, but no amount of comfort, no amount of handholding, could offset the doctor's deadly diagnosis: she had a cancerous tumor pressing on her brain. According to my aunt Lee, via cousin Ruth, my mother had suffered from severe headaches from the time she was thirteen. To help her get through these throbbing, head-splitting episodes, my mother would sit in a dark room rocking back and forth until the pain subsided. At the time, everyone in my mother's family believed her headaches were the product of her "sensitive" and "artistic" nature and that over time she would outgrow them. Given the state of medical knowledge in the 1920s and 1930s, my family's view of my mother's malady is understandable. As it turned out, her headaches became more severe as she grew older as the undetected tumor grew ever larger in the fertile darkness inside her skull. (Upon reflection, it seems to me that my mother was probably not known to be fatally ill until sometime after 1935 or 1936,otherwise I don't think they would have planned to have another child, that being myself, in 1933.)

Chapter Eight

Here are a few memories from my early childhood that I am able to recall with indelible fidelity. As I record these it's as though a switch has been turned on in my head and I am instantly back in time.

Late one evening my sister, about six or seven at the time, was howling with pain from an earache (later diagnosed as mastoiditis). Somehow my father managed to get the home telephone number of the pharmacist who owned the drugstore in our neighborhood. He called him up, got him out of bed, and met him at the pharmacy to obtain medicine to relieve my sister's pain.

Another memory, from when I was about five: my parents, my sister and I were in the living room. I was enjoying a piece of white rock candy on a string when I started to choke. My father immediately sprang up from his chair and turned me upside down and began shaking me and slapping my back until the candy tumbled out of my mouth, to the great relief of my mother as she watched my father perform his version of the Heimlich maneuver (which was not invented until 1974 by Dr. Henry Jay Heimlich).

Despite the hard times during the 1930s,my father occasionally came home from work with a surprise for my sister and me. I remember these special evenings very clearly. He would walk through the front door of our apartment, hang up his coat and hat, greet my mother either in the kitchen or in bed (if she was not in the hospital) and then come to us in the living room. He always sat in the same green brocade chair next to a small mahogany end table. He would then invite us to join him, which we did with great anticipation as he removed a glistening Hershey's chocolate bar from his jacket pocket—not just a regular Hershey's bar, but one with almonds inside, wrapped in dark brown shiny paper with silver lettering. With his green pearlized penknife (which he carried with him his entire life), he placed the bar on his thigh and meticulously cut it into three even pieces. The first piece would bear the letters "HER." The second piece would contain the letters "SHE" and the third piece carried the letters "Y'S." As I watched him perform these surgeon-like incisions, I was secretly hoping that the piece I would get would have at least one almond inside. You could always tell where the almonds were because they formed a slight bump under the outside wrapper. Since I could never tell which piece I was going to get, all I could do was wait patiently and try not to show my anxiety. As I figured it, I was either going to be lucky or not. When my father completed the task he would hand one piece to me and one to my sister. Each piece was still inside the paper wrapper. As quickly as I could I would remove the outer wrapper to look for lumps on the surface of the candy bar to detect any almonds hidden inside. As I think about it now, I'm not certain what my father did with the third piece printed with the letters "Y'S." I can't remember if he ate it himself or put it aside for my mother—if she was even home on some of these evenings or in the hospital.

One day late in the afternoon, when I was about five, I was downstairs in the lobby of our apartment house waiting for my father to come home from work. I was impatient to tell him how sad I was feeling, or as he would say, "down in the dumps." When he walked through the large, heavy glass-and-wrought- iron doors I immediately ran up to him, and as soon as I reached him my eyes welled up with tears which I had, until this moment, managed to hold back. I remember he knelt down and put his arms around me and asked me why I was crying. With a quaver in my voice I told him how that afternoon I had wanted to buy a piece of penny candy at Max's candy store, but I didn't have any money. My father comforted me and told me not to worry any more. He said the next time I wanted a piece of candy all I had to do was tell Max I wanted credit. I had no idea what credit meant, but if my father said it would work, I believed him.

Max's candy store was located at the bottom of the street, around the corner from our apartment house. The store itself was on the street level, underneath an apartment house similar to ours. Over Max's front door, and extending over two large showcase windows, one on each side of the door, was a dark green canvas awning with Max's name printed on it in white letters. Also printed on the awning were the words "newspapers," "magazines," "cigars," and "stationery." When you walked into Max's you would invariably find him behind the counter enthroned on a tall wooden stool next to a majestic-looking cash register which, itself, sat imperiously on top of a thick glass countertop. I can't ever remember walking into Max's store when he was not in this exact spot and puffing on a cigar. It was only out of necessity, so it seemed to me, that he would make the effort required to get up from the stool in order to retrieve a box of cigars for a customer, or some stationery supplies (like a Parker or Waterman fountain pen), or a gift-wrapped box of Schrafft's Chocolate or Whitman's Samplers, or when a child like me wanted to purchase a piece of penny candy which was displayed neatly in glass trays behind cloudless glass panes low enough so kids could get a good look at the entire selection.

The day after my father told me to use the magic word "credit," I went down to Max's to test out my father's plan. I remember I was somewhat nervous, fearing that Max wouldn't understand what I meant when I asked for credit. What if he asked me, "What's credit?" I wouldn't know what to say. Nevertheless I was eager to test my father's plan. So I walked into the store and immediately went over to where the penny candies were on display. After a few seconds I looked at Max who, as always, was perched on his stool smoking a cigar near his prized possession, his cash register. I said, "I'll have a Baby Ruth, please."Max slowly slid off his stool and sauntered toward the candy display. From behind the counter he opened one of the sliding glass panels and reached in for a Baby Ruth. He slid the glass panel closed, handed me the candy bar, and said "That'll be one cent." I looked him right in the eye and said, "I want credit."

He responded mellifluously, "Sure, sonny, for you anytime" and then casually strolled back to his usual nesting place. I was in total disbelief. Not wishing to remain in Max's presence any longer than I had to, for fear he might change his mind, I walked out of the store. I couldn't believe it. I had just gotten a candy bar without paying for it. I was filled with unalloyed relief and joy about what had just happened.

Needless to say, I didn't waste any time devouring my magically-obtained candy bar. It was only years later I figured out that my father, who stopped in at Max's store every night on his way home to pick up his evening paper, the *World-Telegram & Sun*, would reimburse Max for my occasional confectionary indulgence.

Like a lot of kids, I believed that the Baby Ruth candy bar got its name from Babe Ruth, the famous 1920s baseball player who was a member of the world champion New York Yankees. Even though the Babe never publicly denied the association, the little known truth is that the candy bar was named after President Grover Cleveland's daughter, "baby Ruth," who, along with her father, had visited the Curtiss Candy Company manufacturing plant some years before Babe Ruth was a national hero—largely for establishing the single season home run record, hitting sixty of them in 1927 (a record not to be broken until 1961 when Roger Maris of the NY Yankees hit sixty-one homers).

Another memory: I was downstairs playing with my friend Leonard in front of my apartment house. I was about five at the time. We each had a wooden spinning top. Mine was painted blue and red. To make it spin you had to carefully wrap the string around it, beginning at the narrow end at the bottom, where the metal tip was, and work your way up the wider part. Then you'd set the top down on the ground, with the metal point touching the cement, and pull the string as fast and as evenly as you could to make it spin under its own power once it was free of the string. Suddenly Leonard, without any provocation that I can recall, slammed the pointed end of his top into my scalp. I instinctively put my hand to my head. When I looked at my hand I saw it was stained with blood. I got scared. I grabbed my top and my tricycle and headed down the cement walkway along the side of our building. At the bottom of the ramp there was a courtyard surrounded on three sides by the walls and windows of our building. Kids would often stand in the center of the courtyard and look up at the windows of their apartment and call out "Ma." Of all the "Mas" in the building only that child's mother—recognizing her child's voice—would come to the window and look down into the courtyard.

With tears running down my cheeks I stood patiently waiting for my mother to come to the window. After what seemed like an eternity she came to the window and looked down at me. I yelled up at her, "Leonard hit me in the head with his top." My voice resonated with urgency, but my mother didn't even open the window. She just looked down at me, her face close to the pane. She wore a sad expression and motioned to me to come upstairs. At that moment I felt a flush of anger. I didn't care that she was sick. I wanted her to come down and get me—now, this minute. But she couldn't, and she didn't, and there was nothing I could do about it. So I walked through the basement door of our apartment house, struggling with my tricycle which, at that moment, I hated, because it was giving me so much trouble as I dragged it behind me to get it on the elevator so I could go upstairs.

The apartment house we lived in at that time, 1746 Andrews Avenue, was across the street from the headquarters of the Salvation Army, whose rolling hills were protected by a cement wall topped by a tall wrought iron fence with sharp-tipped spears. Down the street and around the corner from our building was University Avenue, the main thoroughfare in that part of the Bronx where most of the shops were located, including Rushmeyer's, an ice cream emporium where you could get, as a special treat, a charlotte russe for five cents. To reach our apartment house you had to walk up a hill. If you were an adult carrying bundles of groceries, the hill could be a challenge. However, if you were a kid the hill made for exhilarating sledding, or "belly-whopping" as it was called. At my young age, around six, I can only remember sledding down it once. Perhaps the fact that I never did it again has something to do with a murky memory I have of a car swerving and skidding up the hill, narrowly missing me, as I was swiftly gliding down.

During the summer, mothers would set up their colorful, collapsible beach chairs and sit in their flowered housedresses under the mid-day sun with their backs against the high wall surrounding the Salvation Army grounds. Here they would while away a few hours in the afternoon, enjoying each other's company, before it was time to go upstairs and prepare dinner for their families. No matter how engaging the conversation was, these women managed, as only mothers can, to keep a watchful eye on their children who were busy playing a variety of games on the sidewalk in front of them. From time to time, without interrupting the flow of neighborly conversation, they could easily respond with a reassuring smile to the shouts from their own child, who was performing some special acrobatic feat while yelling, "Watch me, mommy. Watch me." Young girls mostly played jacks or hopscotch (also called potsie) or they jumped rope while reciting a rhythmic chant which always began with the letter A in the alphabet:

> A, my name is Alice
> My husband's name is Al
> We live in Albany
> And we sell apples.

Because it was too much trouble to go upstairs to visit the bathroom, most mothers would help their children, little boys and girls, to pee in the street next to the curb. I can't recall my mother ever engaging in this practice.

One afternoon, for whatever reason, my mother, sitting in her beach chair, decided it was time to go upstairs. In the Bronx, if you lived in an apartment house, you never went "home." You always went "upstairs." On this particular day my mother had forgotten her key to the lobby of our apartment house. A neighbor friend of hers, who lived in the adjoining building, allowed my mother to use her key to get into the lobby of her apartment house. Once inside we took the elevator to the top floor, walked up one flight to the roof, and crossed over the parapet to the roof of our house. In the Bronx, apartment houses were built within inches of each other, so it was relatively easy to slip over a low wall to get from one roof to the other. All went well until we got to the wall. I managed to get across easily enough. So did my mother, until she took her first step on our roof when her foot caught on a wire and she fell to the ground with a thud. I immediately ran over to help her get up, but she was unconscious. I started yelling, "Mommy, get up, get up. Please, Mommy, get up." But she didn't move. I ran for the big metal fire door on the roof that opened up to the stairwell. Fortunately the janitor of our building was half a floor below on his hands and knees (with a bucket of soapy water and a brush) scrubbing the stone steps. I remember grabbing him by the arm and trying to pull him up the stairs to the roof at the same time that I was trying to tell him what had happened."Please help me," I said." "My mother fell on the roof and I can't wake her up."He quickly ran ahead of me to reach my mother. I remember he carried her downstairs to our apartment. He must have used a passkey to open the door; I can only assume the janitor waited around until my mother regained consciousness before he left.

In 1995, the last time I visited my old neighborhood, the Salvation Army building had been converted into the South Bronx Job Corps which, according to a faded sign on the front lawn, offered "Free Vocational Training for Youths 16 to 21." Also, our apartment building had been torn down and with callous disregard for my memory, so it seemed to me, had been replaced by a parking lot. Max's candy store was also missing. In its place I found Lee's Fish Market and La Javilla Food Plaza, and in front of these stores were shiny black cars with black-tinted windows and young men with dark glasses leaning on fenders smoking cigarettes.

There was further desecration to the world that existed in

my childhood. Around the corner on University Avenue, next to P.S. 82 where my sister first attended grammar school (which is still there), only the shell of the Park Plaza movie theater remained—the very same theater where my cousin Lenny had worked at as an usher while attending high school; the same theater where my sister and I, with at least a few hundred other kids, watched, on a Saturday morning (without parental supervision) a live puppet show of Jack and the Beanstalk.

The theater, with over two thousand seats, was built in 1927 and played double bills of second run films. It closed in 1964. Gone, too, were the retail shops that had surrounded the theater in the late 1930s, like Murray Gold's Antiques, Sylvia's Greeting Cards and the Cotton Plaza, a women's clothing store. In their place and along the front of the building, where the theater's marquee originally hung overhead, and the ticket booth had been located, now stood street-level shops including Key Food, Glenis Restaurant, Plaza Pizzeria and the University Laundromat.

I remember standing stock-still in front of these unfamiliar businesses and asking myself, "What am I feeling?" At first I had difficulty identifying the precise nature of the discomfort I felt. But then it struck me. It was an acute sense of longing; longing to be back in time when my parents were still alive and Max's candy store was still open for my penny business. I longed for all of it as I pictured it in my mind. I longed for the innocence and simplicity of my childhood and the security I had felt when both my parents were alive, including the thin strand of hope that my mother "would not be sick anymore" and we would all be happy.

It was a bright, sunny Saturday morning, late spring or early summer, probably 1937 or 1938. My mother was in bed wearing a lightweight, floral-patterned bathrobe and a cotton bonnet to cover her bald head which had been shaved in the hospital before her most recent operation. I was standing at the head of the bed near my mother. Next to me was a teenage girl who lived on our street. My mother was giving her instructions about where to take my sister and me for a day's outing. I remember my mother's weak voice mentioning something about a boat ride to Bear Mountain (a popular state park about fifty miles up the Hudson River from Manhattan). Then my mother reached over for her purse on the night table next to her bed. She took out some bills and handed them to the girl and said, "Make sure they have a good time."

It was about this time that my father hired a woman to clean the house and help take care of my sister and me. She may even have done some cooking. I don't remember. Her name was Hattie Mae. She was a large black woman whom I liked very much and felt safe with when we left the house to run errands. I remember one time we had to take a trolley to get someplace and a man attempted to jostle his way in front of me as I was about to step up onto the trolley. Without any hesitation Hattie shoved the man aside so I could board the trolley car. Hattie slept on a cot in our foyer, and every morning she would fold it up and store it in the hallway closet.

Another memory. It was late afternoon. My sister and I were alone in our parents' bedroom in our fifth floor apartment on Andrews Avenue. (I say alone, but I'm not certain that Hattie wasn't somewhere in the apartment.) We were leaning on the windowsill in front of the window that looked down on the street. After a while the room grew dark and slightly chilly, yet neither one of us moved from our spot to turn on a light or get a sweater. Gradually we got used to the darkness and although we didn't say anything to each other, I think we both felt (at least I did) that it was fitting to sit in the dark, as though we had a premonition that something bad was about to happen. I don't know what thoughts were running through my sister's mind as we remained motionless in front of the window staring out onto the dark, rainy street below looking at the glistening lamp-post lights, the marquee that festooned the Park Plaza movie theater, the bright red and yellow wooden trolley cars and automobiles moving along the wet pavement on University Avenue. As for myself, I was secretly hoping to spot my father down there on the street because then I would know he would be home any minute. Even on a clear day, when it was still light, I doubt I could've seen him, let alone recognize him, or anyone else. But searching for him gave me something to do, something to distract me and help keep my fear at bay.

Finally I heard the key to the front door of our apartment turning in the lock. I knew it had to be my father. Moments later I heard him walk into the living room. Then I heard his footsteps approaching the bedroom. He came into the room and without saying a word, and without looking at us, he turned and stood in front of a dark mahogany dresser. I noticed that he had a brown paper bag in his hand. I watched him as he removed what looked like a drinking glass, but the glass was filled with wax, and there was a small wick sticking up in the center. My father placed a white handkerchief on his head, then lit a match and touched it to the wick. It quickly caught fire. We watched our father in the dark as he slowly placed the glowing glass candle on top of the dresser. He then turned and walked toward my sister and I. He gently placed his arms around both of us and said, "Your mother has gone away on a long trip and won't be coming back." My sister began to cry. I watched her sobbing and wondered why she was crying.

I remember thinking that my father had stated a simple fact. He had told us the truth the best way he knew how. He said my mother was gone and wouldn't be coming back and that was that. I remember feeling sorry for my sister because she seemed so upset, but I couldn't see what good crying would do. In that moment I felt I had no choice but to accept what my father had just told us as an unalterable fact of life, and I knew that nothing in the world could change what had happened; nothing could be done to bring my mother back. A few years later I did come close to tears when I saw Walt Disney's *Bambi* (d: David Hand, 1942) and heard Bambi's father, The Great Prince, tell his son that a band of hunters had killed his mother, saying "Your mother can't be with you anymore." Like my father and the Great Prince, many parents during this era avoided the use of the words "death" or "dead," and certainly never mentioned the word "cancer," when explaining the loss of a parent to their children.

The difference that a mother's emollient presence can make in a child's life is described in Agatha Christie's autobiography: ". . . the solace and strength of [her]mother's love and understanding when there was trouble. In the black abyss of misery, holding tight to her hand had been the one comfort. There was something magnetic and healing in her touch. In illness there was no one like her. She could give you her own strength and vitality." Experiencing such motherly love is unimaginable to me, and has left a void in my psyche that altered my life forever.

From the moment my sister and I learned of our mother's death I think we instinctively called upon our own resources to survive the devastating blow that turned our world upside down. In that moment we were brought face-to-face with the fact that we live in an unpredictable and unsafe world, and at our tender ages we were handicapped by not having words or images to process this earth-shattering event. Abraham Lincoln, whose mother died when he was nine, wrote that sorrow comes "with bitterest agony" to the young because it "takes them unawares." The finality of such an event takes the breath away and leaves one at a complete loss for words. It is too catastrophic to make sense of. When Mark Twain learned (by a cablegram which reached him in Europe) of the death of his beloved twenty-four year-old-daughter Susy, he wrote of the incident in his autobiography: "It is one of the mysteries of our nature that a man [let alone a mere child], all unprepared, can receive a thunder-stroke like that and live." Over time my sister and I learned, each in our own way, to survive our mother's death and make our way in the world, but make no mistake about it, the separate paths our lives took, for better or worse, whether we were (or are) aware of it or not—were shaped by this tragedy.

Looking back on my life, I think I inherited my artistic sensibility from my mother and my resoluteness from my father, and most certainly my view of the unpredictability and impermanence of life has been etched in my psyche as a result of my mother's death. Over time, I became an agreeable sort, eager to get along and fit in, but always scanning the horizon for danger, always looking for side doors and exit signs. Like my father, I became a keen observer of human nature. These qualities became tools to help me navigate the world.

My sister followed a different path to survive this trauma. She became decidedly self-sufficient and a rationalist—sometimes an extreme rationalist—in an attempt to protect her tightly controlled world view that rejected any seemingly irrational behavior, and I think she experienced our mother's death as the ultimate act of irrationality since she had no words to explain it. In retrospect, it seems to me my sister also reached the conclusion that, in order to survive in an uncertain world, she would be better off controlling all aspects of her life herself, and not relying on anyone else for help or comfort, because they might not be there when you need them. Most family members and friends, I think, view my sister as a kind and generous person who, at times, can be maddeningly "head-strong" or "strong-willed," but also someone they, and I, love dearly. The two different survival paths my sister and I embraced, are often cited as common trajectories that children may follow who have lost a parent.

The candle my father undoubtedly purchased on his way home from the hospital was a yahrzeit memorial candle. In the Jewish tradition you light a candle to observe someone's death. My father was not a religious person, but I think he needed some gesture or symbol to mark the passing of his wife, the mother of his children. According to the official Certificate of Death issued by the Department of Health, Borough of Manhattan, my mother was forty-three when she died. (My father was fifty-three.) The same certificate stated that my mother entered Presbyterian Hospital on West 168[th]Street on June 3, 1939, almost one month before she died there. The time of death is listed as four a.m. on Saturday, July 1, 1939. Knowing my father, I believe he would have visited my mother every day after he finished work, sometime around 5 or 6 p.m. But this was Saturday, and he only worked a half day.

This is what I imagine happened when he showed up at the hospital for his regular afternoon visit on that day. Since he knew where her room was, he probably went directly there only to discover that her hospital bed was empty. Because he had been on the road from early morning (I don't remember us having a telephone in our apartment at the time), there was no way the hospital could have contacted him before his visit. My father, I'm certain, would have been devastated when he was told by one of the nurses on the floor that his wife had died at 4 a.m. that morning. I can only imagine the remorse he must have felt at not having been with her at the end, holding her hand, comforting her, telling her he loved her. On his way home he must have stopped to purchase the yahrzeit candle.

It was exactly two months after my mother's death that newspapers around the country published the news that Germany had invaded Poland in a blitzkrieg attack that lasted only four weeks before Poland's unconditional surrender. Bialystok, with more than 50,000 Jews, some of them undoubtedly relatives of my mother's family, were swept up and never heard from again. Closer to home, several months before my mother died, newspapers reported that 1,200 would-be storm troopers from the German-American Bund had celebrated Hitler's fiftieth birthday at a South Bronx beer hall plastered with swastikas and the slogan: "One People, One Bund, One Führer."

Having survived the Great Depression, my sister's two mastoid operations, the birth of a second child at the peak of unemployment, my mother's torturous death, the threat of civil disobedience (or disturbance)by Nazi-loving German-Americans, and the threat of a looming world war, my father must surely have felt that the forces of fate were conspiring against him, testing his courage and physical endurance. I imagine that my father assessed the situation like a game of cards; if you were lucky you were dealt a good hand; if you were unlucky you were dealt a lousy hand. In either case you did the best you could with the cards you were dealt. More importantly, as I observed him, he played out his hand with a straight face, never feeling sorry for himself. More than once he said to me, "It's a good life if you don't weaken."

Chapter Nine

Almost immediately after my mother's death, my father made arrangements with Aunt Lee and Uncle Leon to shelter my sister and me, at least until he could decide how best to care for us. According to Cousin Ruth, my mother had asked Aunt Lee to help care for us kids in the event she died.

When my sister and I moved in with Aunt Lee she was living in Sea Gate, a moderately up-scale gated community surrounded by beaches at the western tip of Coney Island in Brooklyn, and populated (at that time) mostly by Jewish families living in one or two-family homes. To be sure, my aunt and uncle were not among the well-off families, but we never wanted for food or comfort. During the winter months they rented an apartment there and during the summer months my Aunt Lee operated a fifteen-room boarding house just two blocks from the beach. It was, I suppose, the poor man's vacation resort, because directly across the street, with as many as one hundred rooms, was the splendiferous Ocean Breeze Hotel adorned with green and white canvas awnings. Under the awning, on the side of the hotel facing the ocean, was a long porch lined with plush cushioned rocking chairs to provide guests with the ultimate in comfort as they watched the sun set over the Atlantic on warm summer evenings, or observed guests playing croquet on the hotel's well-groomed front lawn. The hotel's owner, Mr. Gershenoff, a man devoid of warmth or social graces, occasionally patrolled the porch to make certain that no uninvited guests (like me) were enjoying themselves at his expense. He had good reason to guard the porch because one evening (I think it was 1941) I did sneak up and peek through an open window into a large room which on Thursday evenings was transformed into a movie theater. The movie I watched—without getting caught—was *Golden Boy* (d: Rouben Mamoulian,1939), starring Barbara Stanwyck and William Holden.

Sea Gate, this sandy strip of paradise, was off limits to the working-class residents living in Coney Island and the thousands of visitors who came from all over the New York area every summer to enjoy the amusement park rides and escape the heat in the refreshing waters of the Atlantic.

At my aunt Lee's boarding house I often crawled under the front porch to look for coins that fell between the wooden floorboards. In the dark, with a flashlight in one hand, I would dig on my hands and knees in the damp sand trying as much as possible to avoid spider webs and the crawling or flying insects whose habitat I was willing to invade in my search for riches. Mostly I found pennies, nickels, and sometimes, dimes featuring a silhouette of Mercury, who, to my eyes, always looked more like a goddess than a Roman god. If I were really lucky

I might come upon an occasional quarter or half-dollar piece engraved with a picture of Lady Liberty

Later on, when my father sent me off to Sea Gate for the summer, my sister, my cousin Ruth and I, would sleep on small fold-up cots inside a cottage at the side of the boarding house. As I recall there was one bare bulb inside, powered by electricity from the main house using an extension cord. At the time it didn't matter to me where I slept because after a full day of running around like a "wild Indian," (as my aunt would describe my daily adventures), not even damp sheets with a residue of gritty sand could prevent the onset of sleep.

One early Saturday morning I slipped out of the house unnoticed with a box of pretzels tucked under my arm for breakfast. I was anxious for another summer day to begin, so I strolled over one block to the beach, which was deserted at this hour. I started walking along the water's edge munching on my pretzels and taking pleasure in leaving a trail of footprints at the water's edge. Soon afterwards I saw a man walking toward me. Just as we were about to pass each other, he told me—as he pointed his thumb over his shoulder—there's a dead man down there lying on the beach. "A dead man," I said to myself. "I've never seen a dead man," so off I raced. Pretty soon I came upon a few policemen standing over a sodden body they had dragged out of the water. The man's face was misshapen and purple and his stomach was grossly distended. He reminded me of Fatsuff, a humorous Hawaiian character in the Similin' Jack comic strip whose belly was so huge he kept popping the buttons off his shirt. I stared at the man a long time to satisfy every bit of my curiosity. Soon, one of the police officers shooed me away. I remember running back home at top speed to wake up my aunt and uncle and report breathlessly about my encounter with a dead man.

*　*　*

Aunt Lee was a smallish woman—no taller, I believe, than five two. She had short-cropped salt and pepper hair, boundless energy and walked with a tomboyish gait. According to my cousin Ruth, my aunt Lee was bold and daring in her youth. As one family story goes, she was caught stealing pennies from a blind news dealer—probably a spur of the moment prank or a response to a dare by one of her friends. When she was older she was arrested for attending a political rally for Eugene V. Debs, the leader of the Socialist party. In 1918 Debs was sentenced to ten years in prison for denouncing the government's prosecution of prominent Socialists who opposed U.S. involvement in World War I. In 1921 President Warren G. Harding pardoned Debs and saved him from wasting away in an Atlanta prison. By the time I came to live with her, Aunt Lee had given up political activism and was committed to a new cause: bringing in extra money to help support her family—which she did by working part-time for her older brother, Murray, selling gimcracks in his second-rate gift shop in a black Brooklyn neighborhood. While she may have given up active involvement in political causes, I don't think she ever gave up her interest in social justice. During World War II she took me to see a stage play (I think it was *Native Son*) performed in a small Brooklyn theater starring Canada Lee, a celebrated film and stage actor who pioneered roles for African Americans and helped champion the advancement of civil rights in the 1930s and 1940s. I remember one of the actors reciting a line about "this incestuous bed." Upon leaving the theater I asked Aunt Lee what an incestuous bed was, but she didn't give me an explanation I could understand.

My uncle Leon was a portly, genial man before he suffered a stroke in 1952; he eventually died on March 2, 1956 at the age of fifty-two. Two things he dearly loved, besides my aunt Lee and his daughter, were his El Producto cigars and listening to opera on the radio. He especially loved the Metropolitan Opera radio broadcasts on Saturday mornings, hosted by Milton Cross whose sonorous voice was a familiar hallmark to opera lovers.

Uncle Leon was the youngest child in a family of six or seven children (one or more remaining in Europe) who was pretty much left on his own to grow up. It is possible that his parents were so tired out after having raised so many children before him that they no longer had the energy to raise one more child. One of his siblings became a doctor, one a dentist, one a college professor, and another, a sister, became (or at least aspired to become) a concert pianist. It's family lore that her public recitals were vanity performances paid for by her wealthy brothers, whose generosity did not extend to my uncle Leon. It could well be that this early childhood neglect was a contributing factor in my uncle's failure to achieve the level of success that his brothers and sister did.

Uncle Leon did not continue his education beyond high school and made a modest living as a short-order cook, mostly in luncheonettes. As a member of the culinary union, he would be sent out to work at different eating establishments, most of them small, family owned and operated. Virtually every new job he started would begin auspiciously. He would come home and tell my aunt Lee how nice the people were at work and how much they appreciated his skill and knowledge. However, in a matter of weeks or months the honeymoon would end as my Uncle offered advice to the boss about how to improve the business. This was advice the owners didn't need to hear since they had been getting along just fine before my Uncle arrived on the scene. Invariably they would fire him. He would complain to my aunt that the head chef was inept, or the boss was unreasonably demanding, or that he wasn't being paid enough for all the work he did. "They couldn't run that place without me," he would stubbornly insist.

This pattern continued throughout most of his working life—whether working as a short-order cook or selling pickles out of the back seat of his car—and earned him the reputation in the family—much to my aunt Lee's chagrin—of not being "a good provider." As far as I was concerned, on one Saturday morning, he did prove himself to be a good provider. I had previously asked my aunt for money to go to the movies and she had turned me down. When I left the house—dejected, I might add—I found my uncle sitting on a bench outside. I told him Aunt Lee wouldn't give me money to go to the movies. He immediately dug into his pocket, pulled out a quarter, and handed it to me and then said, "But don't tell your Aunt Lee I gave you the money."

Based on a clumsily phrased but tender and loving inscription he penned inside a book of poetry he gave to my aunt Lee, it's obvious that my uncle adored her, or at least he did early on in their marriage. But according to Ruth, his adoration was unrequited. She told me that his inability to earn a decent living made it difficult for her mother to return his love. Instead, she felt "suffocated" by his display of "sentimental" affection.

My maternal grandparents circa 1905. Ida and Soloman Sampson. Children from left to right: Leah (Aunt Lee) Frieda, Murray and my mother, Florence. (Kate, the oldest, is not in this photograph.)

My mother at age sixteen.

My mother in her late twenties, circa 1921.

My mother, sister and I on the beach in Sea Gate, circa 1936.

My sister and I in our parent's apartment on Andrews Avenue in the Bronx, circa 1937.

My sister and I on the beach, circa 1938.

Park Plaza movie theater, circa 1938. Courtesy of The Bronx County Historical Society

My father showing one of his inventions to Uncle Harry, circa 1947.

My father in front of Aunt Lee's apartment in Sea Gate, circa 1944.

Chapter Ten

Saturdays, especially rainy Saturdays, were good days to go to the movies. With this objective in mind I would initiate my "complaining routine," directed at my aunt Lee (when I was living there permanently, or spending part of my summer vacation there). My most effective complaints were "My life is boring" and "I have nothing to do," which by design placed the responsibility for my day's entertainment squarely on my aunt's shoulders. Despite her many suggestions, I found a host of puerile reasons to reject them. Just about every kid I knew agreed that if you sustained this whining long enough, adults would eventually become exasperated and reluctantly agree that the best thing for you to do was to go to the movies. This premeditated assault on my aunt's nerves often elicited the anticipated response, "Here, go already"—at which point she would find her change purse and gladly hand over the price of admission, with the parting remark, "I have too many things to do around the house, and I can't get them done if you're going to be under my feet all day."

The only time I remember this ploy not working was during one summer in the 1940s when there was widespread fear of a polio epidemic, and parents were cautioned not to send their children to crowded movie houses where they might become infected.

One Saturday around noon, as I had done dozens of times before, I walked to the Surf movie theater in Coney Island . I can't remember exactly how old I was at the time—probably nine or ten. It was a small theater that played films two or three weeks after they ran in the larger theaters in the neighborhood. The price of admission was eleven cents—at least it always had been, up until that day. I walked up to the ticket booth and passed my eleven cents under the glass window. The lady inside the booth said:

"The price is fourteen cents."

I told her she must be mistaken. "I always pay eleven cents."

She said, "The price went up."

I asked her, "Who said so?"

She said "The owner."

I said, "He can't do that."

She said, "Yes he can, sonny. He's the owner and he can raise the price anytime he wants."

I was dumbfounded. I had never heard of such a thing. I thought that prices, whether for the movies, candy, ice cream, whatever, always remained the same. Since I saw it was futile to argue with this woman, I paid her the fourteen cents and walked inside the theater, but my mind was spinning. I couldn't comprehend what had happened. I tried to sort it all out in my head. I thought if you owned a movie theater, drug store, candy store or a bakery (all the places where I usually spent money) maybe you just woke up one morning and said, "Today I'm raising the price," and that's all there was to it. Maybe you talked it over with your wife first, but that's all. After that, you went to your place of business and told your customers "Today we have a new price." However, as soon as I got inside the theater and bought my candy (probably Good 'N Plenty), I settled into my seat and lost myself in the images being projected on the screen.

During the summer months I went to the movies a lot. In those days theaters didn't bother to list the times movies started. People just walked in any time, even if it meant arriving in the middle of a movie. At some point you'd realize you had already seen a particular scene, at which time you would say to your friend or date, "Isn't this where we came in?" At that point you'd get up and leave. Many times you didn't even know what movies were playing. You just went.

On Saturdays I'd arrive at about noon and wouldn't leave this darkened pleasure dome until about four o'clock. As I exited the theater I would squint at the glare of the sun and face the heat of another endless summer's day. Inside the theater, however, time passed quickly and my eyes remained fixed on the screen as I watched a double feature, at least one cartoon (usually starring Donald Duck), and a weekly movie "serial." When I was a kid we called them "chapters." These "serials" were a cinematic art form like no other. They were, as my friend Ken Weiss, author of *To Be Continued*, reminds us, a unique movie genre that defied any sense of rationality. Week after week these action-packed episodes would keep us on the edge of our seats, all of them ending with a cliffhanger scene to lure us kids back to the theater the following week to see how the hero escapes almost certain death. During the 1940s, there were literally hundreds of different serials, some featuring established comic book heroes, and others inspired by popular radio shows, and still others created out of the producer's unbridled imagination. What they all shared in common were plots as insubstantial as Jell-O, performed with absurd eclectic costumes, inane dialogue and chintzy sets. What they lacked in artistic merit, they made up for with action that included ridiculous fistfights and ingenuous destructive devices such as trap doors, death rays, landslides, booby traps, explosions, and dozens of crackpot diabolical schemes that seemed to make no sense at all. Most of the serials were produced by Hollywood B studios and independents on "Poverty Row" because there was not enough profit in them to warrant attention by the major studios. If you're as old as I am, you may remember some of them from the 1940s: Don Winslow of the Navy, 1942; Captain Midnight, 1942; Batman, 1943; Captain America, 1944; Jungle Queen, 1945; The Royal Mountain Rides Again, 1945; Hop Harrigan, 1946; Superman, 1948.

In addition to these thrilling movie serials, there usually was a Fox Movietone newsreel (narrated, if I remember correctly, by Ed Hirlehy), and possibly an international bike race. These races were like horse races at the tracks, only instead of riding horses the athletes from virtually every major country in the world were riding bikes. On these special Saturdays when bike races were shown, a uniformed usher at the door would tear your admission ticket in half, and then give you a small card with a number printed on it. The numbers matched the numbers worn by the cyclists. Naturally, you rooted for the racer wearing your number. If he finished first you'd take your number to the manager's office and receive a prize.

From the very beginning until the end of the race, which usually lasted around four or five minutes, virtually every kid in the theater was screaming and yelling—some standing on their seats—cheering their designated racer on to victory. What made these bike races so exciting was that there were no rules. And since there were no rules or judges in evidence, each rider was free to use whatever dirty tricks he could think of in order to win. It was not unusual to see an Italian racer kick a German racer off the road into a mud hole, or a Frenchman stick a tree branch in the spokes of a bike of a Chinese rider. If your athlete was the Chinese rider you moaned and yelled, "Foul, foul," and quickly lost interest in the remainder of the race because your chances of winning a prize had just ended up in a ditch somewhere along the mountainous course. These aggressively competitive tactics took place until there were just a few riders left coming down the home stretch. Eventually one rider breezed across the finish line before the others, and the kid holding the lucky matching number would run up the aisle to the manager's office to claim his prize, which wasn't much as I remember—but, in those days, a prize was a prize.

The bike races eventually disappeared, mostly because they were illegal. They were considered a lottery because they required a person to pay money (the admission price to the theater) to take a chance (on which bike rider would finish first) to win a prize. If these three elements (chance, consideration and prize) were present, the game or promotion was considered a lottery or sweepstakes, which was illegal. It just took the government a little while before it cracked down on this game of chance. On certain other Saturdays when you entered the theater, you might be given a free out-of-date comic book, maybe Terry Toons, Classic Comics, Police Comics or All-Star Comics with the top third of the front cover having been removed. I assume the removal of part of the front cover made it legal for local newspaper and magazine wholesalers to re-sell "damaged" issues to movie houses at cut-rate prices.

On many Saturday visits to the movies I usually brought a sandwich in a brown paper bag hidden under my jacket to get around the theater's prohibition against bringing food inside. I would usually bring a bologna or salami sandwich on Wonder Bread slathered with French's yellow mustard. Of course it was perfectly permissible to eat candy that you purchased at the candy counter in the lobby —a permanent fixture in movie theaters ever since the Great Depression, when theater owners were desperate to find new sources of revenue. During the show, if you got hungry, and wanted to take a bite of your sandwich, you'd bend down behind the seat in front of you to avoid being spotted by one of the prowling matrons, usually middle-aged women dressed in starched white uniforms and armed with large flashlights to spot offenders. To avoid getting caught, you waited until the matron walked by your row, like a sentry on patrol. I always thought of these eagle-eyed matrons as part of an elite corps of Nazi guards who patrolled the aisles to prevent us from eating our lunch, or to make sure we didn't put our feet up on the seats in front us, or to break up any fights that might break out. Their job was made easier because on Saturday afternoons all kids had to sit on the right side of the theater so as not to disturb any adults sitting in the middle or left sections. For good reasons, not too many adults attended Saturday matinees with a bunch of kids either booing or hissing at bad guys on the screen.

Chapter Eleven

During our first summer in Sea Gate, my father had time to collect his thoughts, and to place all of our household furnishings in storage. I can only imagine how difficult this must have been for him, to box up all his earthly belongings and ship them off to a cold, impersonal warehouse. It must have broken his heart to pack up our dishes and silverware, the pots my mother cooked with and the pans she used to bake with. The pictures they hung on the walls of their apartment. The sheets and pillow cases from their bed. And then to go into the bathroom and pick up her hair brush and her comb, and even her toothbrush and lipstick, and put them in a paper bag and somehow dispose of them, maybe toss them into the garbage. And at some point he had to go into their bedroom and go through the dresser they shared and handle her clothes, especially her underwear and all the intimate memories they contained. For him this must have seemed like Act Three of Death's tragic drama, when the curtain comes down and the protagonist knows, for a fact, that the best years of his life have just ended and he is on his own once again.

Even though he was forced to place all our furnishings in storage, I believe it was always his dream that one day he would reclaim them and at the same time reclaim his children and re-build his family. Until that time, he would do whatever he could to keep his family intact. This is how it came about that in the fall of 1940, my sister, myself, and our father moved in with the Cohens, a warm Jewish family who owned a home in New Rochelle, close to my father's business territory.

It all started with Mrs. Cohen's best friend, Mrs. Shottner.

Mrs. Shottner and her husband owned Shottner's kosher butcher shop on Lawton Street in New Rochelle. As I remember it was a small store. They served customers in the front and killed, cut, and dressed chickens in the back. The floor in the front room was covered with a combination of saw-dust and chicken feathers. Mrs. Shottner, draped in a white, bloodstained apron, sat on a low stool next to the meat case holding court with her women customers as she simultane-ously plucked feathers from the warm, limp bodies of freshly killed chickens.

As the story goes, my father told Mrs. Shottner that his wife had recently died of cancer and that he had had little choice but to send his two children off to live with his wife's sister in Brooklyn. What he really wanted, he explained, was to have his children live with him but he didn't know how he could manage this all by himself on his modest income and with no one to look after my sister and me during the day.

Mrs. Shottner told my father's story to Mr. Cohen who

owned a wine and liquor shop next door, and he repeated the story to his wife. Knowing Mrs. Cohen, this gracious, warmhearted woman must have said something like, "That's dreadful. Something must be done about this. We must help this poor man and his children." Mrs. Cohen, a mother of three grown sons, took action, and it soon came to pass that she invited my father, my sister, and I to come live with her and her family at an affordable price for room and board—an act of unusual generosity and personal inconvenience I only came to fully appreciate after I was married and had children of my own.

Mr. and Mrs. Cohen owned a green and white colonial-style home at 78 Rhodes Street, where they raised three sons: Howard, a doctor; Eugene, a loving son (but a hellion at eighteen) who married well and went to work for his father-in-law; and Myron, fifteen, also a loving son and very studious. At one time, all three boys had slept in the attic, but by 1941 Howard had married and left home, Eugene continued to sleep in the attic, and Myron slept in a bedroom next to his parents' bedroom on the second floor. By the time we arrived at the Cohens' home, Howard and Eugene were away from home in the armed services fighting World War II. My father, sister and I slept in an adjoining bedroom. We took all our meals with the family. Mrs. Cohen kept kosher and was a fabulous cook. A year later, an incident occurred that sent my sister and me back to Sea Gate. My sister, ten years old at the time, told my father, "Myron kissed me." Years later my father told me he felt that the best way he could protect her from any further adolescent mischief was to send her back to Aunt Lee. I can't remember why my father sent me back with her, but he did.

In Sea Gate, when the summer season ended, and the vacationers returned to their homes, the boarding house was shuttered and Aunt Lee and the rest of us moved into a rental apartment at 3831 Atlantic Avenue, directly across the street from the beach. It was a three-story, red brick building that contained four separate apartments. Originally we lived on the ground floor. My sister, Cousin Ruth and me all slept on one daybed in the living room. In the morning, after we got up and dressed, my aunt would convert the bed into a couch with decorative pillows in an effort to veil its dual purpose. In addition to sleeping there, the living room was also where we kids sat around in the evenings. During my time at Aunt Lee's, I cannot remember my sister playing with me or looking after me in any big-sisterly way. I knew she was my sister, but in name only, for I didn't feel close to her during our childhood.

Once, I was lying on the floor with my Jumbo Parker crayons busily coloring pictures of cowboys and Indians in one of my favorite Blue Ribbon coloring books. At some point I looked up to observe my sister sitting at a desk across the room with her back to me. There was a small lamp on the desk and several opened textbooks. It was obvious my sister was doing her homework. Even from the back I could sense how hard she was concentrating. I simply stared at her back and wondered to myself, *How does she know what she's doing?*

Because I was acutely aware of my inability to catch on quickly to whatever was being taught at school, I was all the more impressed with my sister. I saw that she was able to figure things out on her own in a way I couldn't. The idea of applying oneself, that is, studying, could produce learning, was a concept that never occurred to me. I simply accepted the fact—with Cousin Ruth's concurrence—that Lucille was the brains in the family.

When I think of learning in the academic sense, or in my case the lack thereof, I'm reminded of the following story. One day a grandfather decided to walk his seven-year-old grandson home after school. On the way home the grandson asked, "Grandpa, do you know the name of the tallest mountain in the United States?" The grandfather said "No." A little while later the grandson asked, "How deep is the Pacific Ocean?" The Grandfather replied, "I used to know but I forgot." A little while later the grandchild asked, "What year was the Empire State Building built?" The grandfather said "I don't know." Then he patted his grandson on the head and said, "Good boy. Keep asking questions. How else are you going to learn?"

During my childhood years I cannot recall anyone ever taking me to a library. And I certainly didn't take myself there. Unlike some kids my age who eventually became writers, I was reading comic books when they were reading the *Hardy Boys* series and later on *Kidnapped*, *Treasure Island*, Kipling's *Jungle Book* series, *Tom Sawyer* and *Huckleberry Finn*, and after that maybe Edgar Allan Poe and Sherlock Holmes and any number of biographies. No, at an early age, I was not a reader which has produced a literary deficiency in me I'm still attempting to overcome. I can't help but imagine what a difference it would have made in my life if I had had the experience described by author Doris Kearns Goodwin in her memoir, *Wait Till Next Year:*

Every night, after I brushed my teeth and settled into bed, my mother came to read to me. I loved listening to her voice, so much softer and less piercing than mine. She read slowly and deliberately, lingering over the passages she liked, helping me feel the rhythm of the language, the pleasure in well-chosen words. She modulated her voice to reflect the different characters and the pace of the narration.

At about this time my aunt, uncle, and we three kids moved upstairs to smaller quarters, after the building's owners decided to make the downstairs space available for either friends or relatives. Given my aunt and uncle's financial situation at that particular time, the move to the attic apartment for less rent was probably a welcome relief. As it turned out we all became good friends with the new occupants, Janet and David Altman and their two little boys, Jeffrey and Danny.

To reach our new apartment one had to climb several flights of winding stairs. At the top, as you turned right, you entered the first room of this two-room apartment. In this room, next to a small kitchen area, was the kitchen table; and in the same room, near a window that looked out on the ocean, was a couch which served as my bed. The second room was used as a bedroom for my aunt and uncle. Down the hall, past the bathroom, was the attic which you entered by ducking your head and taking one step up. Once inside you had to bend your knees in spots to keep from hitting your head on the slanted wooden beams that supported the roof. Undoubtedly this attic room was intended for use as a storage area, but Aunt Lee fixed it up as a bedroom for my sister and my cousin Ruth.

Early in 1941, my father and Aunt Lee had a dust-up . At the time I was a short, eight-year-old kid, skinny as a pencil. On one particular Sunday visit to Sea Gate I sensed that something was bothering my father. He probably had been worrying about me for some time until he could no longer contain himself. He made some sort of comment to the effect that he was worried about how thin I was and that maybe Aunt Lee wasn't taking proper care of me.

His awkwardly phrased expression of parental concern apparently hit a nerve in Aunt Lee, and set off a firestorm of anger in her. After a few moments of heated words, my father began retreating down the stairs and narrowly missed being hit on the head by a pot my aunt hurled at him in her fury. (In all fairness to my Aunt Lee, I never did gain much in height or weight, weighing only 118 pounds when I enlisted in the Navy at the age of eighteen.)

My sister and I followed my father downstairs to a wooden bench In front of the house. The three of us sat down, with my father in the middle. He turned toward my sister and asked her if she would like to return to New Rochelle so we could all live together. Without any hesitation, she told him she would rather remain with Aunt Lee in Sea Gate. Then my father turned to me and asked me the same question. Having heard my sister's response, I knew my father was hurt, and I also knew he would be doubly hurt if I, too, told him I didn't want to live with him. Even though I was happy living a carefree life in Sea Gate, and probably would have preferred living there, I couldn't say no to him. The moment my father asked the question, I distinctly felt his pain as though it were my own. Because I couldn't bear to inflict any additional suffering on him, I readily agreed to move back with him to New Rochelle.

Maybe the following story will help shed some light on my sister's strained relationship with our father.

When we were both middle-aged adults my sister confided in me that she felt our father was a strict disciplinarian, an opinion she formed at a very young age, perhaps seven or eight (when our mother was still alive) based on one of rare childhood memories. She told me she recalled our father coming home from work one day and saying to my sister and me, "If you don't behave yourselves I'm going to take off my belt to you children."

Even if my father had threatened us, as my sister recalls, knowing him as well as I did, I think that any threat he may have made more than likely was motivated by his love and concern for our mother, since, at times, she was barely able to take care of herself, let alone to take care of two small children. Because he was concerned about her health, I can imagine him asking our mother, when he returned home from work, "How do you feel?" "How was your day today?" "Did the children give you any trouble?" In this context it's possible he may, on occasion, have warned my sister and I to behave ourselves, not to cause our mother too much trouble or he would take his strap off to us. Seen from this perspective, it would seem he was more interested in *protecting* our mother than *punishing* us. Without question, this would have been a difficult insight for any eight-year-old child to grasp, no matter how smart she was in school.

What is so ironic about all this, is that my sister admitted to me that, when her patience wore thin by her own children's tomfoolery, she would often take a wooden spoon from the kitchen drawer and threaten them. When I asked my sister's daughter, Shelli, if her mom ever actually hit her or her brother with the spoon, she said, "Yes. She'd give us a couple of whacks. Nothing that would fall under the heading of child abuse, but enough to restore peace and quiet in the house." In my conversation with Shelli she reassured me, of what I already knew: "We love our parents and both of us turned out just fine."

At some point—I can't recall the exact chronology—my Aunt Lee moved around the corner from the apartment on Atlantic Avenue. The new dwelling was located on Surf Avenue. It was a darkish sub-basement apartment. The windows in all the rooms were small and located close to the ceiling so when you looked up you saw the shoes and ankles of people passing by. The apartment had two bedrooms, one for my aunt and uncle and one for my sister and cousin Ruth.

When Ruth was 82 I asked her—during her annual Thanksgiving visit to our home—about her teenage years growing up with my sister. She told me that that period of her life was very difficult to discuss, including her belief (not entirely unfounded from what I had observed) that her mother loved Lucille more than she loved her, her own daughter—or at the very least admired Lucille's intellect, personality, and ambition more than cousin Ruth's. A bitter pill for any teenager to swallow! My sister didn't make life any easier for Cousin Ruth at this time. Although at home they got along like sisters, outside the house Ruth was pretty much on her own without any close girlfriends, and my sister, according to Ruth, didn't make room for her in her circle of friends—but this all by itself is not uncommon between siblings, or near siblings. The friends my sister made were bright, attractive teenage girls from moderately well-off families; the kind of friends who made it possible for her to create a new world for herself, one that was free of impediments or memories that could cause her further pain and suffering, or stand in the way of making a success of herself.

From inauspicious beginnings, Ruth managed to create a pleasant life for herself. Over time she made some very dear friends and derived great pleasure from living with and caring for her mother as she grew older. "I'm so glad I had those years with her," she told me. "We really bonded." She also found fulfillment in her job of many years as a travel agent in Las Vegas, where she lives to this day.

My sister's subconscious determination to erase just about all memories of her early childhood is not, so it would seem, uncommon behavior among survivors of childhood trauma. I can readily call to mind two notable examples. One was Rudyard Kipling, who was psychologically and emotionally abused by the elderly married couple (mostly by the fanatically religious wife) who were retained to raise him and his younger sister in England, while his parents remained in India enjoying a relatively comfortable lifestyle in the service of the government. In Kipling's case, he was able to assuage his unhappy childhood by creating imaginative tales about young boys endowed with heroic qualities (e.g., Kim, Mowgli), who were either orphaned or abandoned.

The other was Charles Lindbergh whose parents were wholly incapable of showing affection. By the time he was ten his parents had formally separated but kept the separation a secret to protect his father's reputation as a Republican congressman. Growing up, Lindbergh divided his time between Little Falls, Minnesota, and Washington D.C., and consequently felt unsettled in both locations— much the way I did shuttling between the Bronx, Sea Gate, New Rochelle, and then back again to the Bronx. According to Bill Bryson in his book, *One Summer*, Lindbergh and his mother never hugged. At bedtime, they shook hands. "Lindbergh himself in adulthood said that he had no memories at all of his daily life as a youngster. In his first autobiographical effort, called *We*, he gave just eighteen lines to his childhood."

When I was living in Sea Gate in my Aunt Lee's Surf Avenue apartment, or spending the summer there, I slept on a fold-up cot in the living room that my aunt made up for me every night. The sub-basement apartment was in a red brick three-family home located diagonally across the street from the Ocean Breeze hotel. The owners of the building, the Levyns, lived on the first floor with their two young adult daughters, Sherry and Bernice. The Franks family lived on the top floor.

By this time my father had patched things up with Aunt Lee, and he continued to visit my sister and me in Sea Gate most Sundays. I remember how I looked forward to his visits. On many occasions he would sit on the couch reading me the comic strips in the *Sunday Daily News*. On one of his visits, I explained to him that I had lost my collection of baseball trading cards—about thirty of them—in a game with several boys. The game was called flipping, and the object of the game was to flip your card to the ground to match the other boy's card. If the side with the picture of a ballplayer was turned up, you had to match it. If it landed with the picture face down, you lost and the other boy would pick up his card and yours. After I told him my story my father walked me to the candy store just outside Sea Gate and gave the store owner a one dollar bill. Since one picture card came inside each package of bubble gum, at a cost of one cent each, I instantly came into possession of one hundred brand new baseball trading cards, a bonanza by any kid's calculation. When we got back to Aunt Lee's house, I quickly opened many of the gum wrappers to find out which ball players' pictures I had been lucky enough to acquire. Printed on the front of each card was a photo of a ballplayer. On the back was printed the player's biographical information (height, weight, birthplace), the team he played for, and his batting statistics. I was always looking for players from the Brooklyn Dodgers, like Dixie Walker (outfielder), Pee Wee Reese (shortstop), Pete Reiser (outfielder), Cookie Lavagetto (third base), Dolph Camilli (first base), and so on. They were called trading cards because kids would frequently trade one card for another, especially if a kid had doubles or triples of the same card which he was willing to swap to get a card he didn't already have.

Bubble gum card-collecting days began in 1933 when the Goudey Gum Company first inserted cards in packages with a stick of gum. With the outbreak of World War II, bubble gum became as scarce as professional baseball players who went off to war. In the 1950s and 1960s, as the number of baseball clubs expanded, card collecting had a resurgence of popularity among kids when Topps company began inserting baseball cards in its packages of gum. Before the era of bubble gum baseball cards,

tobacco manufacturers, as early as the 1870s,were distributing them to stiffen their packages and promote their cigarette
brands, including American Beauty, Fatima, Mecca, Old Judge,
American Tobacco Company, to name a few. During the years
1909-1911 baseball cards, today valuable collector's items, featured such celebrated players as Ty Cobb, Honus Wagner and
Christy Mathewson.

As the years passed, my sister barely acknowledged my father when he showed up for his Sunday visits. She didn't greet
him with any sign of affection. No hug or a kiss. Nothing. At the
time, I couldn't understand this. He was our father and I loved
him, and I couldn't understand why she didn't feel the same
way. In retrospect, I think at the core of my sister's dissatisfac-
tion with our father was embarrassment over his age and his lack
of formal education. More than likely, he didn't measure up to
her girlfriends' fathers. I'm sure my father must have sensed her
disaffection but he never mentioned it to her or to me. As I look
back on my sister's behavior, I think she did what she felt she
had to do in order to survive the tragic loss of our mother and
get on with her life in the best way possible. For my part, I have
long since let go of any resentment I felt toward my sister when
we were growing up.

My "letting go" reminds me of a story from the Zen tradition that makes the point that in this transitory life we should
try to live in the present moment, and not hold on to the past.
The story begins when a Zen master and his disciple are walking
through the woods on their way to a monastery where they in-
tend to spend the night. Along the way they come upon a beautiful young maiden in distress. She wishes to cross a muddy stream

but is afraid that she will soil her stylish kimono and silk slippers. Without a moment's hesitation, the Zen master stepped forward and lifted the young woman in his arms and carried her across the stream. He put her down gently, and after she thanked him, the master continued on his way with his young disciple in tow. That evening, as the pair were preparing for sleep, the disciple addressed his master: "Pardon me, master, if I am speaking out of turn, but we monks have taken vows never to touch a woman. How could you have picked up that woman this morning?" The master reflected for a moment on the disciple's remark, and then replied: "Young man, I put that woman down early this morning. You are still carrying her around."

At a minimum the Sunday visits from New Rochelle would easily take my father two-and-a-half-hours each way. First he would take the New York Central railroad from New Rochelle to Grand Central Station. Then he would take the shuttle from Forty Second Street to Times Square to catch the Sea Beach Express which would take him to the last stop, Stilwell Avenue in Coney Island. Then he boarded a trolley car and took that to the last stop, Norton's Point, which left him one block outside of Sea Gate and another few blocks from Aunt Lee's home. On most Sundays my father stayed for an early dinner. For these meals my aunt would move the table out of the kitchen and into the living room where there was more room. After dinner he would start the long trek back home.

On some Sunday afternoons, before dinner, my uncle Leon and Uncle Lou (who was married to my mother's older sister, Aunt Frieda), and a neighbor, Mr. Koening, would play a game of pinochle. On one of these Sundays my father caught my Uncle Lou cheating and called him out on it. Angry words were exchanged. My father made no bones about the fact that he didn't like or trust Uncle Lou and neither did I. He was always making wisecracks at our expense, and often ridiculed Cousin Ruth and treated her with contempt.

Later on, after I had moved back to New Rochelle, I would make this arduous trip with my father. Upon arriving at Grand Central Terminal we walked up a ramp and entered the main concourse with its twin marble staircases and vaulted ceiling. In the center of this cavernous hall, sunlight pouring in through steel-ribbed skylights, was a glass-enclosed information kiosk with a clock, facing in all four directions, mounted at the top. Along one wall of the concourse tellers sat behind glass panels selling tickets. On the opposite side of the concourse, were the gates one passed through to reach the tracks where trains arrived and departed. Grand Central Station was originally constructed in 1913 as "a triumphant portal to New York." Eighty-five years later, in 1998, it was scrubbed clean of decades of grime and restored to its original magnificence.

During the trip home my father would agree to sit in the first car of the Sea Beach train so I could stand up and look out the front window as the train sped by station after station on its way to Manhattan. The motorman who ran the train sat next to me sealed up in a tiny steel cubicle, barely big enough for one person. Peering through the large glass window in front of me, I had fun pretending I was steering the train with him as we hurtled through the darkness, the tracks illuminated by the train's head lights. Inside the tunnels, red and green lights told the motorman whether to proceed or halt. The close tunnel walls created the sensation that the train was traveling much faster than it actually was.

One Sunday evening, much to my disappointment, my favorite spot at the front window was occupied by a young man and his girlfriend. The young man had his arm around the girl's waist under her jacket. I watched them from the back as they talked and laughed and occasionally I noticed he gave her a squeeze. And then I observed something odd; something that positively puzzled me. His hand slowly slid down and rubbed her behind. I was fascinated by this move and the smoothness with which it was carried out, with no objection coming from the girl. For the life of me I couldn't figure out why he would want to do such a thing, or why she would let him touch her behind, which I thought would be off limits to any man. I knew something funny was going on but I had no idea what it was. My only wish was for them to get off at the next stop so I could get my place back in front of the window.

When we reached 42nd Street and embarked on the last leg of our journey on board the New York Central, my father would usually doze off on the much more comfortable seats. I would either read a comic book or practice drawing on an artist's pad I had brought along. My "drawing" consisted of copying, not tracing, pictures of Walt Disney characters like Mickey Mouse or Donald Duck and his nephews Huey, Dewey and Louie. Many of the conductors knew us as regular Sunday evening passengers and stopped to talk to us for a few minutes as they punched our tickets. If they saw me drawing they would make some remark to my father about my artistic talent. "That kid of yours sure can draw. You watch, some day he's going to be a famous artist." I knew they were just being friendly and I accepted their compliments graciously. I also knew I was not really drawing. I was only copying pictures from a comic book. Nevertheless, there was something about art that interested me and eventually came to play an important part in my adult life.

It was at Grand Central Station, when I was eight or nine, that I first became aware of how important I was in my father's life. How my very existence was like a tonic to him that seemed to invigorate his otherwise empty life. At age fifty-five I gave him a reason to live: he had a son to raise. This insight—still vivid in my memory over seventy years later—came to me one Sunday when my father walked me over to the information kiosk and introduced me to the agent, a man named Chester, whom my father had become friendly with over the years. He seemed to me a pleasant man with wavy gray hair and a cherubic face. As we approached the kiosk where Chester was seated behind an open window, my father put his arm around my shoulder and said—with a pronounced sense of pride and affection I can still feel this very moment— "I want you to meet my boy."

Chapter Twelve

When I returned to New Rochelle to live permanently with my father in Mrs. Cohen's house, it was sometime in 1942, when I was about nine. World War II had broken out. Only Myron remained at home and attended Isaac Young High School where he was an A student—which impressed me, but didn't inspire me to follow in his footsteps. Part of me wanted to excel academically, but another part of me believed that I didn't have what it would take. Three years later Myron graduated from High school and went on to Cornell University; he eventually became a successful patent attorney.

The following memory will make it clear that I was not prepared to follow in Myron's footsteps. The grammar school I went to when we lived with Mrs. Cohen (the same one Myron had attended) was just three blocks from our house on Stevenson Boulevard, so I always arrived home from school before he did. One day I was waiting impatiently for Myron to arrive home from school so I could share a fascinating, almost unbelievable, nugget of information I had learned in school that day. After he arrived home, and treated himself to a glass of milk and cookies Mrs. Cohen had left on the kitchen table, I told him my astonishing news.

I said to him, "Did you know there is a place in the world called Aunt Jemima, just like the pancake mix?"

"Impossible," he said.

"It's true," I replied. "My geography teacher pointed right to it on the map."

"There has to be some mistake," he said calmly, at which point he walked into the living room to retrieve the World Atlas. "Show me," he said.

I started flipping through the pages. I said, "I know it's here someplace. I'm pretty sure it's around the Black Sea and the Mediterranean."

At this point Myron took the Atlas from me and carefully inspected the pages. Then he pointed his finger to a spot on the map near Turkey. He said, "Here's your Aunt Jemima. Only it's not Aunt Jemima, dummy, it's Asia Minor."

Many years later, when we were both in our fifties, I visited Myron in his Manhattan law firm and he apologized for having called me a "dummy."

Not only was I unprepared to pick up the baton of Myron's intellectual legacy, I was also unprepared to pick up his clarinet, which he had played in the school band at Stephenson Grammar School. In high school he turned his musical attention toward the piano, a talent he used , with his friend Jules, to compose the words and music for several songs for their graduation-night student production.

At the beginning of my new school year Mrs. Cohen generously offered me Myron's clarinet and insisted I join the school band. I accepted her invitation graciously, but secretly I was terrified that I would never be able to learn how to play it. I was having enough difficulty in school without additional pressure. What made matters worse was that this particular clarinet was the top of the line. Other kids in the band had thinner, less expensive models made of polished chrome. The clarinet I was bequeathed came in a black leather case with a blue velvet interior. It looked like the one that Benny Goodman played. It was made of fine, highly polished wood with a black veneer and shiny bright silver keys. By virtue of some administrative process I was not privy to, I found myself enrolled in the school band which met after school several days a week. To this day I believe there was an assumption made by the music teacher that all kids who wanted to be in the band (and I did not) already knew how to play the instrument they brought with them. That is to say, if called upon, they could at least play scales and a few simple songs, and were probably receiving private lessons at home.

As the weeks passed I was never called on to perform, and more importantly, I was never given one minute of instruction. Nevertheless I continued going to band class because I was embarrassed to tell Mrs. Cohen and my father that I could not play the clarinet. To hide the truth I developed what I thought was an ingenuous method of deception. While the others kids were actually playing their clarinets, I put the instrument to my lips, imitated their finger movements, and turned the sheet music when they did. Naturally, I was a nervous wreck. I was just waiting for the moment when the teacher would uncover my ruse.

As the Christmas holidays approached, we began working on a selection of music to be presented to the entire student body in the auditorium the day before Christmas vacation was to begin. And so we practiced. At least other members of the band practiced. I just sat in my seat and continued my charade. One morning, about a week before the performance date, the music teacher planned a dress rehearsal in the auditorium. One by one we picked up our instruments and marched through the halls. We took our seats on gray metal folding chairs right down front below the stage. The band rehearsed one song and all went well. Then the music teacher tapped his baton on the podium to call for quiet and announced we would perform Adeste Fideles (O Come, All Ye Faithful). I then heard him say, "Stephen Zimmerman will lead us in this number." I knew immediately that the jig was up. The moment I had dreaded was upon me. As I began to stand up a million thoughts raced through my mind. Most of all, I thought, *How am I going to get out of this one.* I was surrounded by about thirty kids who were all staring at me. I had no recourse, I thought, but to tell the truth and take my chances. In a moment of surprising bravado I thought to myself, *What's he going to do? Shoot me? Take me to the principal's office. Big deal.* So I addressed the music teacher in as confident a voice as I could muster under the circumstances and said,

"I can't."

He said, "You can't what?"

I said, "I can't lead us in Adeste Fideles."

He said, "Why not?"

I said, "Because I don't know it."

What I didn't tell him was that I didn't know any songs at all, and I certainly didn't know how to play the clarinet. But further explanation didn't seem necessary. I sensed he had all the ammunition he was looking for. The thought crossed my mind that I could tell him I was Jewish and it was against my religion to play music associated with a Christian holiday. But I quickly discarded this gambit because I realized I would only be digging myself into a deeper hole. In a threatening tone, the music teacher said, "Young man, come here. I'm taking you to the principal's office." This was easier said than done. To leave my seat I had to squeeze past several of my classmates sitting in my row. For whatever reasons (not ruling out the possibility of anti-Semitism, since I was the only Jew in the band), they did not make my exit easy. One after the other they impeded my progress by pressing their knees against the back of my legs to make my passage as difficult as possible. Having successfully survived this knee-jabbing gauntlet, I followed my teacher up the center aisle of the auditorium toward two swinging red leather doors. Despite my grim expression, which I feigned for the sake of my classmates and teacher, for whom this was all very serious business, I was having fun pretending that I was a death row prisoner in a gangster film being led to the electric chair.

To this day I don't remember what punishment, if any, I received at school. Nor do I recall how the news of my unpardonable behavior and dismissal from the school band was received at home. All I knew was that I was finished for good with the clarinet and that I would never have to pick it up again. The biggest relief of all, of course, was that I no longer had to pretend I could play the damn thing.

However embarrassing this experience was, it didn't shatter my self-confidence. I simply realized that playing a musical instrument was just one of many things in life I felt I was not suited for. And I let it go at that.

If my father or Mrs. Cohen had asked me if I wanted to study the clarinet in the first place, I would have told them "No," and saved them, and me, a lot of trouble. You see, about a year or so before I moved back to New Rochelle, when I was living in Sea Gate with Aunt Lee, I had made an attempt to take up a musical instrument that had also ended badly. I kinda remember the first time I heard Larry Adler play the harmonica on the radio—I think it was when he made a guest appearance on the Jack Benny show. I was greatly impressed. He was the harmonica virtuoso of his day who could play popular songs and classical pieces with equal ease. In my desire to achieve instant fame among my peers, I thought to myself, *I can do that*. And if I did, I could carry my harmonica around with me in my back pocket. Then, at the drop of a hat—as I envisioned it in my fantasy—I could nonchalantly remove it from my pocket and begin playing to the astonishment of everyone in earshot. Without doubt, I thought, this would make me the most popular kid around.

Somehow I managed to save enough money to purchase a Hohner harmonica. I didn't bother going to a music store. I probably didn't know such a store existed. Instead, I walked to the nearest Woolworth's about two miles away. As soon as I walked out of the store I began to practice. I figured, *how difficult could this be?* I exhaled and inhaled trying desperately to bring forth the melodies I heard swirling around in my head. I couldn't come close! As I walked back home I continued huffing and puffing on my Hohner harmonica until my cheeks began to ache. By the time I arrived home I was exhausted. It never occurred to me to take music lessons because a voice inside my head told me it wouldn't help. I was convinced that the harmonica and I—as well as all other musical instruments—were not destined to share a future together. My own personal maxim at the time was, If at first you don't succeed, quit.

Chapter Thirteen

Rhodes Street, and the surrounding neighborhood, were lined with arching trees that canopied the streets during the summer. For the most part the families in the area were either working class or middle class and most of them were of Italian, German or Irish ancestry, either Catholics or Protestants. Other than the Alperts, who lived about eight houses down the street, and one of Myron's friends around the corner, there were no other Jewish families in the area that I was aware of. The Alperts had two children, Jerry and his sister, Sally. I never felt a real kinship with either one of them, and for good reason. Jerry was a year older than me and was forever trying to get me to do things I didn't want to do.

For example, at Halloween he talked me into stealing a loose-jointed cardboard skeleton from Woolworth's, the kind that hangs on your bedroom door and allows you to move the arms and legs into all sorts of different weird positions. The heist was set for an afternoon after school. At Jerry's prodding we walked over to the counter where the Halloween gimcracks were on display. I remember Jerry looking around furtively, like some two-bit crook in a B movie. In a hushed voice he said, "Now. No one's looking. Just slip it under your jacket." I hesitated. Jerry persisted, saying, "For cryin' out loud, no one is going to see you. Just take the thing and let's go." So I did, but reluctantly.

That evening at dinner, and the following evening as well, I felt too guilty to eat. I sat morosely at the table watching my father and Mr. and Mrs. Cohen eat their dinner. After dinner, on the second night, my father took me up to our room and asked if anything was troubling me? Was there anything on my mind I wanted to talk about? I was grateful for the invitation and freely unburdened myself, confessing to the crime I had committed. After hearing my confession my father asked where the skeleton was that I had stolen. I retrieved it from the back of the closet in our room where I had hidden it. My father did not get angry. Instead, he explained to me that what I had done was wrong and that the only way to correct the situation was to return the stolen merchandise to Woolworth's, which we did that evening. When we got to the counter where the skeletons were on display, I took my stolen item out of a brown paper bag and placed it back on the counter. As soon as I did this my father asked me if I really wanted to have one to hang up in our room. I told him I did, so he told me to pick out the one I wanted and then gave me the money to pay for it at the checkout counter at the front of the store.

Mrs. Cohen had fine, silver-gray hair which she wore in a bun. For reading she wore thin wire-rim glasses which left two small red marks on either side of her nose. Even though she was a stranger to me, I could sense her love and genuine concern for my well-being. She personally took it upon herself to "fatten me up." She was an excellent cook and made sure I always had plenty of wholesome food to eat. She also fed me one teaspoon of Maltine every morning before I left for school. It was a dark brown syrup concoction of molasses, fish oils and vitamins as thick as axle grease that passed slowly down my throat.

In my mind Mrs. Cohen was the image of what the perfect Jewish mother should look and act like. Mr. Cohen, on the other hand, was endowed with a mercurial nature. At home he was generally quiet, but every once in a while he would lose his temper, usually sparked by something I did. When he barked at me his face would turn red and his dark, black bushy eyebrows seemed to come alive. At those times he scared me, and I have every reason to believe he scared the crap out of his own sons when they had misbehaved when they were my age. He was a much different person when he was in his retail store. Here he was talkative and joked around a lot with his helper, Mr. Mc-Cuffy, a thin Irishman I always suspected of drinking too much. When it was slow in the store, Mr. Cohen often worked on *The New York Times* crossword puzzle.

There were aspects to Mr. Cohen's leathery disposition that I couldn't reconcile. He was very religious and, in my innocence, I expected a religious person to be kind and warm-hearted like Mrs. Cohen. Not that I ever saw him do anything overtly mean or utter a disrespectful word to Mrs. Cohen or Myron, but I couldn't square his brooding silence and quick temper with his devotion to God. Every morning at around 7 a.m. he would stand in a corner of the living room and daven—recite the morning prayer. I observed him fleetingly on more than one occasion as he swayed back and forth and mumbled his prayers with the stiff black thongs of the phylacteries strapped to his left arm, and the little black box strapped to his forehead. Draped over his shoulders was a blue-striped, silk prayer shawl. The house was hauntingly silent at this hour, and I knew better than to make noise or cause a disturbance that might interrupt his communion with God for fear of receiving one of his furrowed-brow stares. In retrospect, it is clear to me that underneath his gruff exterior, Mr. Cohen was a kind and loving human being. After all, Mrs. Cohen couldn't have invited my father and I to move in with them—in a room right down the hall from their bedroom—had Mr. Cohen not agreed, even if reluctantly, to the arrangement.

The Cohens' home had a spacious living room. In one corner stood a Philco console radio. Thumb- tacked to the wall directly above the radio was a world map. Mr. Cohen had worked out a secret code with his son, Eugene, to track his whereabouts on board ship during World War II. Eugene's destinations were communicated in his letters home. By writing down the first letter of every fifth word Mr. Cohen could chart his son's oceanic peregrinations from one port to the next, from one battle to the next. Off the living room there was a formal dining room that hadn't been used much since the war began, except for Passover dinners with Mrs. Cohen's relatives. There was a large kitchen toward the rear of the house. Mrs. Cohen kept a two-slice toaster on the kitchen table. Above the table, on a crescent-shaped shelf, was a small radio usually tuned into one or another soap opera. Two of her favorites, as I recall, were *Aunt Jenny's Real Life*

Stories, sponsored by Spry, a vegetable shortening, whose virtues were extolled by the matronly Aunt Jenny herself, and *Big Sister*, sponsored by Rinso laundry detergent. The announcer, Jim Ameche, would open each show over the sound of a tower clock striking: "Yes, there's the clock in Glens Falls Town Hall telling us it's time for Rinso's story of *Big Sister*."

Let me digress here for just a moment to describe two distinct memories that just popped into my head from my New Rochelle days.

I was about eight or nine years old when I had my tonsils removed at Mt. Sinai Hospital. After spending a long, scary night alone in a large, darkened ward, my father appeared early the next morning to pick me up and bring me home. The nurse on duty told my father I would not be able to eat for quite a while, but if I wanted anything at all to soothe my parched throat she suggested ice cream. As soon as we got outside the hospital and into my father's truck, I asked him for a chocolate ice cream cone, which he bought for me at one of New York's ubiquitous candy stores. I was sitting next to him in the front seat. After a few licks of ice cream I promptly threw up on the floor. Needless to say it made a terrible mess, but my father never uttered a word of reproof. He calmly pulled the truck over to the curb, removed a handkerchief from his back pocket and wiped my face, and disposed of the ice cream cone. Then we drove home where he cleaned me up, and then, I guess, cleaned up the truck to rid it of the awful smell.

It was Thursday, April 12, 1945, about 4 o'clock in the afternoon. I was outside playing marbles with a group of my friends when one of the neighborhood kids came running out of his house yelling "President Roosevelt just died." Initially no one believed him, but he swore it was true. "I just heard it on the radio," he said. At that point we all believed him. I quickly grabbed up my marbles and ran into the house for I knew how much Mrs. Cohen revered the president. As usual, she was in the kitchen. Panting for breath I burst out with the news: "President Roosevelt is dead." She gave me a stern look and said, "That's nothing to joke about." (She was all too aware of my puckish nature.) I told her I wasn't joking. "Turn on the radio. You'll hear it." She did, and tears came to her eyes and rolled down her cheeks as she collapsed into one of the kitchen chairs.

Like most Jews, Mrs. Cohen held the president in high esteem, and voted for him repeatedly. Even though he was criticized by some Jews at the time as not doing enough for the Jewish people, especially those in Nazi concentration camps or the refugees attempting to escape the European holocaust, he was seen as friendly to the Jews, and was considered by most American Jews as a better choice than either his predecessors or his rivals.

Back now to Mrs. Cohen's home. Off the kitchen there was a small pantry and laundry room. Also off the kitchen was a door to the basement where there was a Ping-Pong table. On shelves next to the stairwell were Mason jars filled with canned fruits and vegetables that Mrs. Cohen had put up for the winter. A door with an attached screen led directly out of the kitchen into the backyard where there was a flowering rock garden at the rear of the property and a goldfish pond at the center. Each spring Mr. Cohen would go to the pet store and purchase several gold fish. As winter approached, Mr. Cohen would scoop up the fish in a net and place them in a bucket of water. Then he would drive his red, two-door 1940 Pontiac to Beechmont Lake, about fifteen minutes from the house, and empty them in the water where, hopefully, they would survive until spring. In the winter, when the lake froze over, kids from all over the area came to enjoy ice-skating. I tried it once or twice but was never good at it—my ankles kept turning in and after a while they hurt too much to continue. It may have had something to do with the fact that the skates were hand-me-downs from Mrs. Cohen's sons and didn't fit properly. It could also have something to do with the fact that I usually wore slip-on penny loafers that offered virtually no ankle support. One day my father noticed that my ankles turned in toward each other. Shortly thereafter he took me to a podiatrist who prescribed sturdy brown plastic-molded orthopedic arches to be inserted in my shoes to correct the problem. After this my father tossed out my loafers and bought me a pair of unattractive sensible shoes. I wore these with the arches for about a year until my ankles grew stronger and I no longer needed the support. I was happy to get back to wearing fashionable shoes once again that also provided decent ankle support. No more penny loafers for me.

One night shortly after dinner my father and I returned to our upstairs bedroom. At age 57, after a long, hard day at work, he was ready to relax and read his evening newspaper. Since I was sitting in the lone, large, cushiony chair, there was no place else for him to sit other than on the hassock stationed directly in front of the chair. I don't know what possessed me, but at age ten I thought it would be awfully funny if I kicked the hassock away with my feet just before he sat down. This was a prank I would normally play on my friends, but at that moment I was at the mercy of my impulses. Sure enough, just as my father was about to sit down, my legs flew straight out and the hassock knocked my father over. Still holding on to his newspaper, he landed on his backside. Shocked! Stunned!

But not for long. He instantly got himself up off the floor and started chasing after me with the newspaper rolled up like a weapon. I ran out of our bedroom and down the stairs, two steps at a time, all the while yelling back over my shoulder, "Dad, I didn't mean it. It was only a joke." He was still hot on my heels. I reached the living room and turned into the kitchen where I ran right past Mr. Cohen sitting at the kitchen table enjoying a cigarette and a cup of coffee. My father was still in hot pursuit, and I was still yelling back, "Dad, I'm sorry. It was only a joke. I was just kidding." Before my father could catch hold of me I managed to fly out the back door of the house letting the screen door slam behind me. My father did not follow me out of the house. I waited a long time before I felt it was safe to go back inside. By the time I returned to our room my father's anger had dissipated. I apologized and he allowed me to wrap my arms around his neck. Remorseful about the trick I had played on him, I just hung on to him and hugged him for a long time.

Chapter Fourteen

It may have been Mrs. Cohen's influence, reinforced by my mother's sisters living in Brooklyn, that prompted my father to send me to *cheder*, Hebrew School, to prepare me for my Bar Mitzvah at age thirteen, still a year away. To this day I remember my Hebrew teacher's name because it was quite unusual. Elefant was his name, and when spoken, at least to my ear, sounded like the animal, elephant. (This could have been another one of my Asia Minor errors.) I learned to read Hebrew rather quickly, but, of course, I didn't understand a word of what I read. What I did understand was that the Rabbi's twelve-year-old daughter, Barbara, liked me and one day I found myself inside her parents' house, right next door to the synagogue, and with nobody home we began kissing and fooling around. It was all very innocent and I soon left to attend my scheduled afternoon Hebrew lesson with her father, hoping the smirk fresh on my face was not too noticeable when he greeted me. Making out with the rabbi's daughter, in his own house, was a triumph of sorts, but one that I kept to myself.

I was indifferent to my father's decision that I be Bar Mitz-vahed, but went along with it because, without his saying so, I sensed this special occasion (not the ritual itself) was important to him. It was a chance for him to show my mother's family that he was raising his son properly. My Aunt Lee made arrangements for the Bar Mitzvah service to take place in the small synagogue in Sea Gate, followed by a bare bones reception in the basement.

As it turned out, I almost ruined the occasion. To begin with, the lectern I was to read from was so tall someone had to scurry around the synagogue at the last minute to find a wooden crate I could stand on (I think one that had previously held fruit or vegetables from A&P) so I could read from the Torah and Haftorah placed in front of me. I was mortified. I felt like a little kid being forced to sit in a booster seat in the barber shop. At the beginning of the service I read quickly and clearly—with some authority, I might add—even though I had no idea what any of it meant. However, at some point I inadvertently skipped a line and the rabbi, standing next to me, leaned into my ear and said ,"Go back. You skipped a line." In a hushed voice I said to him, "Don't worry about it. Nobody will notice." He whispered to me, "Yes they will. Go back and read the line." I quietly ar-gued, "Don't make such a big deal about one line."He said, "You must read the line or you can't be Bar Mitzvahed." At this point I relented and went back and read the line. Looking back on this incident, I'm reminded of something Voltaire said: "God is a comedian playing to an audience too afraid to laugh."

Because of Mr. and Mrs. Cohen, and my aunts and uncles in Brooklyn—especially my Aunt Frieda who was the most religiously observant member of the family—I felt a kinship with Judaism—not from a theological perspective but on a cultural level. At the very least I was familiar with such Yiddish expressions like *"mishigoss," "mishpokha," "shlemazl," "oy gevalt," "l'chaim,"* and *"Oy veys mir."* Most of all, I was happily familiar with Jewish foods like Hebrew National bologna, salami, and hot dogs with mustard and sauerkraut. On Friday nights challah was served with dinner, after Mrs. Cohen completed her ritual prayers over Shabbat candles. With her hands covering her eyes, she recited the blessing. *"Baruch atah Adonai; Eloheinu melech ha-olam . . ."*

Despite this cultural familiarity, I never felt strongly enough about Judaism to defend its thousands-year-old teachings at the risk of bodily harm from roaming anti-Semitic crusaders (kids my age) who were out to avenge their Lord from "Christ killers" like me. On one occasion several of them ambushed me and tore my Hebrew books from my arms and threw them down a sewer. I didn't feel persecuted as much as I felt bewildered. I tried to make sense out of their verbal assaults and actions, but I could not come up with a satisfactory explanation. I had the feeling they didn't hate me personally for anything I did or said to them. Their anger seemed directed at something apart from me; at some ancient grudge that neither they nor I knew much about. I knew I was a "Jew," but I didn't especially feel like a "Jew." I felt like a kid who was being called names and being blamed for something I had no part in.

The closest I ever came to belonging to an organized religion was becoming a member of the Westchester Ethical Culture Society where I enrolled my two young daughters, Julie and Tracy, in Sunday school. Soon afterwards I became one of the teachers and, eventually, director of the school. I joined the Society after one of my daughters asked me during dinner, "Are we Jewish, Daddy?" I didn't feel it was enough to simply tell her what we weren't. I wanted her and her sister to be exposed to a teaching that replaced religious faith with a code of ethical behavior. The Ethical Culture movement was founded by Felix Adler in New York in 1877. Adler, the son of a rabbi, was a professor of political and social ethics who asserted that the development of moral behavior can be fostered independently of religious ritual and without belief in a supreme deity—a concept Christian fundamentalists and many ordinary church-and temple-goers find difficult to comprehend. Adler died in 1933, the year I was born.

Ultimately I decided that Judaism's culture and wisdom, and especially its humor, had enriched my life. Beyond that I have found it impossible to accept its religious teachings based on the idea of a world created by God—a paternal God who is concerned, and at times actually involved, with the quotidian details of his "children" who follow (or attempt to follow) his stern laws . . . and for those who fall short of the mark, watch out. My wife affectionately refers to me as her "Bagel Jew."

From my perspective, it stands to reason that if there is no personal, interceding God, then prayer (as it is commonly understood) is useless, nothing more than *hope* dressed up in religious garments. Alexander Graham Bell addressed this topic in 1880, as an entire nation prayed in vain for the recovery of President James Garfield who had been felled by an assassin's bullet: "If prayers could avail to save the sick, surely the earnest heartfelt cry of a whole nation to God would have availed in this case." President Garfield died on September 19, 1881, after eleven weeks of fervent prayer.

Speaking of prayer I'm reminded of the following story:

A man from the United States takes a vacation to Israel and one day he visits the Wailing Wall. He stands there for quite a while, watching the men pray. At one point he goes over to an elderly Jew and says,

"Excuse me, how long have you been praying here?"

The man replies: "About forty years."

" And what do you pray for?"

The man says: "I pray that all the fighting around the world will cease. I pray that little children won't get sick and die. I pray that nobody in the world should go hungry."

"What does it feel like to pray here day after day?"

The man says: "It's like talking to a brick wall."

As I entered adulthood I came to the realization that luck—pure dumb luck, good or bad (some people call it fate, accident or even, God help us, a miracle)—has an important role to play in the outcome of our lives. Consider Enrico Caruso, the famous opera singer, who was lucky to escape with his life when the 1906 San Francisco earthquake struck and completely destroyed the Palace Hotel where he was staying. In his *Memoirs,* Tennessee Williams wrote the following: "Success in the theatre came to me pretty late by prevailing standards, but whether good fortune comes to you early or late, if it comes at all, you have to know you've been lucky." When asked what kind of generals he liked best, Napoleon is said to have replied, "Lucky ones." And when Oliver Sacks, renowned neurologist and writer, was told he had terminal cancer, he retorted, "My luck has run out."

Whenever I talk about luck, I am reminded of the following Zen story:

> A farmer had a horse but one day the horse ran away and so the farmer and his son had to plow their fields themselves. Their neighbors came to the farmer's house and said, "Oh, what bad luck you have had." The farmer calmly replied, "Good luck, bad luck, who knows?"
>
> The next week, the horse returned to the farm bringing with him a herd of wild horses. Once again his neighbors came to his house and said, "Oh, what wonderful luck." The farmer listened to their assessment and responded, "Good luck, bad luck, who knows."
>
> The next week the farmer's son was thrown off one of the horses breaking his leg. The neighbors rushed to the farmer's house and bemoaned his bad luck. The farmer thanked them for their sympathy and said, "Good luck, bad luck, who knows."
>
> A short time later the ruler of the country recruited all young men to join his army to prepare for battle. When the soldiers arrived at the farmer's house, they found the young man unable to walk and left him at home. When the neighbors heard what had happened they rushed to the farmer's house and exclaimed, "What good luck that your son was not forced to join the military." The farmer placidly remarked, "Good luck, bad luck, who knows."

It should be noted that, in the Zen tradition, this charming story has a deeper meaning. The lesson that the story hopes to convey is the importance of maintaining a mental attitude of calm acceptance; of not being swept off one's feet by the vicissitudes of external circumstances. Whether good fortune or misfortune come your way, the Zen mind is prepared to take life as it comes. Remain calm. Maintain your balance. Do not rush to judgment. As one Zen master invariably said, when confronted by disturbing or unexpected events, "Is that so!"

My wife, Jean, and I know something about luck. When we met I wondered the same thing Humphrey Bogart did when he met Ingrid Bergman in *Casablanca* (d: Michael Curtiz, 1942). "I was wondering," he said, "why I'm so lucky. Why I should find you waiting for me to come along."

I found Jean thumping watermelons outside Whole Foods in Berkeley, California, at eight p.m. on May 15, 2000. She was a grade school teacher at the time we met. She had never been married and I'd like to believe the Fates were saving her for me. I said as much in my wedding toast on November 26, 2004. "For all the years I lived alone, I was convinced that in my attempts to meet the woman of my dreams, the Fates were conspiring against me. But then when I met Jean, I realized that the Fates weren't conspiring against me during those long, lonely years, but were actually protecting me from making another mistake until Jean came along." From the very beginning we have lived as two close friends, always in touch with each other's feelings, always able to make each other laugh, always ready to listen to each other in times of stress or heart ache. In her *Memoirs*, George Sand expressed this kind of closeness more eloquently than I ever could, when she wrote the following about her son, an illustrator and writer, then in his twenties:

> He and I do not see alike in all matters, but we have kindred constitutions, many of the same tastes and needs, and what is more, so fast a natural bond that no dispute between us can last out the day, nor resist a moment's talking heart to heart. If we dwell in different gardens of thought and feeling, there is at least a large and ever open door in the wall between: the door of immense affection and absolute trust.

Not only were we lucky we met, we were also lucky that we share the same philosophic and religious views—or non-religious views, as it turned out. More than this, we both cherish the working-class values of the 1930s and 1940s that my father and her parents passed on to us. Additionally, I am an avowed atheist, and Jean, in her more nuanced way, prefers to describe herself as a secular humanist. By either appellation, we both agree there is no divine providence watching over us.

It seems to me that we humans are made of the same stuff that the universe is comprised of. For we are not born into this world, but out of it. It further seems to me that all and everything in the universe is in the process of change, struggling to survive in one form or another, either evolving or devolving, or morphing into something entirely new and unimaginable. For humans, survival means not only surviving physically, but surviving as well as possible—emotionally, psychologically, and economically—with the least amount of pain and the maximum amount of pleasure. Although there may not be any overarching purpose to life that we can discern, our lives are nevertheless filled with meaning — tender moments of love and compassion that comfort us, sensations of joy and happiness that make us feel lighthearted, acts of kindness that elicit feelings of brotherly love, intellectual achievement that rewards us with a sense of satisfaction, as well as occasional sorrow and heartache brought on by disappointment, illness and death. The human condition is such that all these things make life meaningful and worth living, that is, for as long as we are healthy enough to enjoy them.

The impulse for survival derives its energy from the same ineffable, complex forces inherent in the universe that are constantly interacting with each other (in a kind of never-ending erotic dance) that pulsates with life at every level of existence. If I were a religious person, I would kneel down before the impulse for survival as the one true God of the universe and the source of all our hopes, dreams and desires—however transitory they may be.

Here on planet Earth, Jean is capable of resonating deeply to the natural world. On one of our first dates I saw that she had a bond with nature that I had never had. We were walking through a neighborhood in the Berkeley hills and stopped in front of a quaint home to admire the garden. I observed the colorful flowers, their shapes and textures and the aesthetically pleasing design. But then I looked over at Jean and realized that a stillness had come over her, and that she was experiencing something I was not. It's as though she had traveled through some neurological pathway to another realm that lies beneath or beyond the surface of things; a realm where humans and Nature come together as one.

Jean loves to be out in the thick of nature tramping along sylvan mountain trails in our country's majestic national parks where, she says, "There's nothing to buy." I do not accompany her on these treks. She usually goes with one of her girlfriends and has a marvelous time. The outdoors is not for me. I did not grow up surrounded by mountains, trees, grass and flowers, but by cement and sturdy, unattractive privet hedges. In New York, trees appear to grow out of sidewalks. As a kid, a stroll through the Bronx (now New York) Botanical Gardens or Central Park was as close as I ever came to the Great Outdoors. On the few occasions when I accompany Jean on one of her walks in a nearby wooded area, I'm always looking around for familiar signposts, like a candy store or bakery, and I have the urge to bring along breadcrumbs to scatter along the way to make sure we can get back to civilization—that is, back to where we parked the car.

Chapter Fifteen

In 1945 my father made a bold move to fulfill a cherished dream.

On April 12th of that year, with World War II drawing to a close, a haggard, sallow-skinned President Franklin Delano Roosevelt returned to his vacation home at Warm Springs, Georgia, where he died of a cerebral hemorrhage. Two hours after his death, with Mrs. Roosevelt at his side, Harry S. Truman was sworn in as the next president of the United States. That same month Italy's fascist leader, Benito Mussolini, was captured and hung, along with his wife, Claretta, in front of a gas station in downtown Milan. On May 7th Germany admitted defeat. The next day the front page of the *New York World-Telegram & Sun*, my father's favorite newspaper, carried the headline: "Nazis give up. Surrender to Allies and Russia Announced." On August 14th Japan surrendered, and on September 2, aboard the USS Battleship Missouri, anchored in Tokyo Bay, the articles of surrender were signed officially ending World War II. Presiding over the ceremonies was General Douglas MacArthur who said, "It is . . . the hope of all mankind that . . . a better world shall emerge out of the blood and carnage."

It was a time for joy and celebration in America. It was a time to look forward to living the good life without food shortages or rationing of sugar, butter and gasoline. Although meat was still in short supply on U.S. dinner tables, the meat industry was promising that this situation would improve shortly. The giant corporations who, five years earlier, had converted their factories into wartime assembly lines to produce ships, tanks, guns and airplanes, were now beginning to gear up to meet the anticipated needs of a victorious America. Mercury and Nash Motors were already advertising their 1946 model cars which they promised would be available soon. Oldsmobile was touting its newest technological breakthrough, Hydra-Matic Drive, and Cadillac encouraged those in the market for one of their prestige cars to get down to their local dealer right away and get their name on a waiting list. Ford placed ads in Life Magazine telling America they'd start up production "whenever we get the green light." Their company slogan was "There's a Ford in your future." Over two million cars rolled off assembly lines the following year. At the same time, the airline industry was making plans to help peacetime air travel get off the ground. Boeing placed magazine ads to tell America that its leadership and experience in the big-bomber field would now be put to use to develop its new Stratocruiser for peacetime air flights. Pan American World Airways meanwhile was giving Americans a glimpse of what they could expect as soon as "conditions permit." What it promised were more spacious aircrafts with first class food service and special smoking and game lounges on board their new Postwar Clippers. Many of the major appliance manufacturers—G.E., Hotpoint, Crosley and Frigidaire—were pitching new, all-electric kitchens with dishwashers and sinks that had their own garbage disposals. RCA was already shipping its new line of postwar radios to retail stores, and television was soon to be our home entertainment center. And with the return of millions of G.I.s, the postwar race to build new homes had begun.

But perhaps the most promising new home of all was envisioned at a June conference in San Francisco when the so-called peace-loving powers of the new world, the "Big Five," laid out plans for the construction of the United Nations. For most Americans it was a time of optimism and pleasure and the makers of Kodak film were telling families to "smile" as they promised that a plentiful supply of Kodak film would soon be available to record the nation's happiness. Major League baseball also got back into the swing of things as big name ball players returned to the game and began crossing home plate instead of crossing enemy lines.

And when returning servicemen weren't listening to a baseball game on radio, they were listening to the swinging sounds of the Big Bands of Benny Goodman, Les Brown, Count Basie, Harry James and Duke Ellington, or grooving to the new jazz sound of Charlie Parker and Dizzy Gillespie called "bebop". At the same time bobbysoxers, my sister among them, were swooning to the sound of Frank Sinatra's romantic voice. Throughout Europe, traitors were being rounded up, tried, and executed. In France, displaced persons forced to flee under Nazi occupation were returning to their homes. And here in America families all over the country were eagerly awaiting the return of their sons and husbands. "My Guy's Come Back," rejoiced Rosie the Riveter.

And back they came, more than three million of them in 1945, some with European and Asian war brides, and others anxious to marry the girls they had left behind. If Americans needed any further proof that the world was once again set aright, they had only to witness the marriage of seventeen-year-old Shirley Temple, America's sweetheart, to Army Air Force Sgt. John Agar. It was a time of homecoming, and a time to be thankful that such a horrible war was over. And perhaps no one was more thankful than General Dwight D. Eisenhower who stepped off an airplane at Washington's National Airport on June 18 and exclaimed, "Oh, God, it's swell to be back." It was a time when families reunited and new families were looking forward to a bright future. It was a time of great excitement and expectations, and my father, I suspect, like almost everyone else, got caught up in the zeitgeist of post-war exuberance.

* * *

On one particular Sunday in 1945 we didn't take the train and subway as usual to visit my sister. Instead, we drove. I asked my father why we were driving to Brooklyn. He said "It's a surprise." Although I didn't know what he had in mind I could tell from the expression on his face that he was in a state of exhilaration. There were only a few occasions when I saw my father giddy with joy, and this was one of them. He definitely had something up his sleeve, a phrase my father was fond of using. I sensed it pleased him, too, that he was able to keep me in suspense. My father's car, which he had recently purchased from a friend of his who owned a used car lot, was a dark blue Chrysler Airflow originally introduced in 1934. It was described as the first automobile aerodynamically designed to minimize wind resistance to offer its owners a smoother, more comfortable ride. This huge, six-passenger sedan my father proudly owned was made in 1937, the last year this streamlined model was produced. Despite its many pioneering features —like automatic overdrive transmission, adjustable front seats, a more horizontal steering column, and extra wide doors for easy entrance, or maybe because of them—it was, in my youthful opinion, one of the ugliest cars I had ever seen. If I had to compare it to something we are familiar with today, I'd say it had the same shape—with its snub-nosed front hood—as a 1960s Volkswagen bug, only ten times bigger. Although my father loved it, I was embarrassed to ride in it. If we passed any of my friends on the street where we lived I would slink down to the floor so they couldn't see me.

When we finally arrived in Sea Gate—some two hours later—my father told Lucille what he had told me, that he had a surprise in store for us. Despite our best efforts to get our father to tell us where he was taking us, he remained silent on the subject. As mentioned earlier, my father and sister did not enjoy a comfortable rapport, and the idea of a planned surprise put her in a restive state. After a brief visit with my aunt and uncle we said goodbye, got in my father's car, and rode off to God knows where. It took us over an hour to arrive at our destination. When we asked where we were, my father said, "The Bronx." He found a parking spot in front of a typical five-story apartment house. It was the last street in the Bronx, 243rd Street and White Plains Road, just before you crossed the line into the city of Mt. Vernon in Westchester County. When we got out of the car, Lucille, already sensing what the surprise might be, asked in a plaintive voice, "Why are we here?" Our father, who could no longer contain his joy, said, "This is where we are going to live. Just the three of us. Like a regular family." From the look on my sister's face, this news was a nightmare come true. To me the idea sounded fine. It's true I enjoyed living in New Rochelle, but if my father said this would be our new home, I was prepared to accept his decision. He was my father. I loved him and trusted him. It was as simple as that in my twelve-year-old mind.

The building he chose was not what you would call fancy. It was a five-story walk-up built prior to the 1920s. Many apartment houses built after that, especially those along the four-and-a--half-mile-long Grand Concourse, were six to eight stories tall and had a modern look to them. Many of them featured stylish wraparound corner windows, sunken living rooms and exteriors composed of cream-colored brick. They also featured impressive Art Deco lobbies. Quite a few had stylishly attired doormen and elevators, and some apartments had as many as five rooms which meant to us kids that the families living there were fairly well off. There was no way my father could have afforded even a one-bedroom apartment, let alone a two-bedroom apartment, in one of these elegant buildings.

Architecturally, the most attractive feature of the apartment house my father had chosen as our new home was the double-tiered courtyard in front. From the street you had to walk up about five shallow but wide stone steps to reach the first court which was either painted or paved with faded red cement. After another twenty steps or so you'd reach another set of five steps that led up to a second courtyard. In earlier times these fashionable twin tiers must have been impressive, especially with the two gray cement planters, each decorated with a sculptured lion couchant, on both sides of the courtyard. Unfortunately, the planters were lacking soil or greenery of any kind, which made the place look run-down. Up the stairs, past the double courtyards, you either turned left or right. If you turned right you entered building 708. If you turned left and walked through two heavy glass wrought iron doors, you entered building 710, where my father had rented apartment 2-B on the second floor.

In my father's deeply-felt desire to bring us together again as a family, he had overlooked the fact that we were no longer small children. The apartment he had selected was identical in layout to the one-bedroom apartment we had lived in on Andrews Avenue when my sister and I were six and eight years old. At age 15, I'm sure my sister would no longer have felt comfortable sleeping on a cot in the same bedroom with her father and brother. I think when my father saw this apartment it made him feel comfortable, as though he were returning home, and without too much thought (which was no match for the power of his emotions at this time) he signed the lease. To complete the picture he had in his mind—of us being reunited as a happy family—he retrieved all of our household furnishings that had been in storage for six years. On the day we arrived he had all the furniture in place. It looked just like the old apartment we had lived in when my mother was alive. As we walked through the apartment we opened closet doors, checked to see if the toilet flushed properly, inspected the medicine cabinet in the bathroom, looked out windows in the front and back, ran the water in the kitchen to see what kind of pressure there was, turned the stove on and off and looked down the dumbwaiter shaft.

In particular, I remember the dumbwaiter. I had never heard of or seen one before. But after we moved in I quickly became acquainted with this primitive contraption. Every evening at about seven o'clock the janitor would stand in the basement and pull on a rope which would run a double-tiered wooden tray up a chute that passed directly behind the wall of every kitchen in the apartment house. After dinner each family placed its garbage in a paper bag, then opened the small door in their kitchen to the garbage chute, and waited until the dumbwaiter arrived at their floor. Sometimes the janitor would miss the opening to the kitchen, and you'd have to yell down to him, "A little higher," or "A little lower," until he got it lined up perfectly. Then you'd place your garbage on one of the empty trays and yell down the chute, "Okay." Then he pulled on another rope to bring the tray down to the basement where he would remove the bags of garbage. He repeated this process until all the garbage in the building had been collected.

But now back to our inspection of the apartment. At a certain point it dawned on my sister and me that there was no place for her to sleep. There was no bedroom like the one she shared with Cousin Ruth in Sea Gate. It didn't take long before anxiety began rising up in me; I was caught between my father's enthusiasm and my sister's brooding silence which made her resistance to the entire enterprise palpable. I could tell she didn't want to be there. Compared to living with Aunt Lee, in the beautiful and tranquil community of Sea Gate, the part of the Bronx my father selected probably seemed anathema to her—a working class environment she had already made up her mind to rise above. Considering the path she had already chosen for herself, living in the Bronx, under the circumstances provided by my father, would have been a turn in the wrong direction. It would have meant giving up her circle of friends in Sea Gate where she felt at home, as well as her close relationship with Aunt Lee and Cousin Ruth. Also, the prospect of living with two men—with no adult woman or my cousin Ruth to confide in—must have contributed to the panic she was feeling. I can't say for sure, because we never talked about it, but my sister may have felt that my father's *surprise* was calculated to trap her into becoming *the woman of the house.*

The upshot of my father's dream ended when my sister—who was totally miserable over the next week or so—left the apartment one night and, on the advice of Aunt Lee, whom my sister called from a pay phone inside Doc Friedman's pharmacy, took a taxi back to Sea Gate. There was so much discord and jangling of nerves on this particular evening that my father either forgot to give her money for the taxi, or he didn't have it to give, or he may have been so hurt and distraught that he refused to pay for it. At any rate, when she arrived back at Sea Gate she asked the driver to wait while she went inside and got the money from Aunt Lee who had somehow managed to scrape up enough cash to pay the fare.

Chapter Sixteen

Despite my sister's refusal to live with us, my father was determined to look after her as best he could. Toward this end he continued the practice of the three of us getting together on Sunday, but instead of my father and I traveling all the way to Brooklyn, it was agreed—now that my sister was a teenager— that we would meet in Manhattan. There were several places around Times Square we staked out as convenient meeting places. We usually met around noon so we could have lunch together, most often at Childs restaurant or Lum's Gardens, a small Chinese place on 53rd Street near Broadway (which I rediscovered by accident many years later when I was working in Manhattan). My favorite eating place was at one of the Horn & Hardart Automats. My favorite dish was franks and beans served in a brown casserole. For dessert it was always blueberry pie which, to my uneducated palate, was as delicious as any that a French pastry chef could have prepared. After lunch my father would treat us to a movie. Depending on the theater, we might also see a live stage show. In those days the really big movies played on Broadway for several weeks in one of the major movie houses, like the Paramount, Capitol, Strand, Roxy or Radio City Music Hall, before being released to neighborhood theaters in the five boroughs of New York.

My father and I allowed my sister to select the movies we would go to because she had very definite opinions about what she wanted to see and because it made very little difference to my father or me what we saw. At the time I was an indiscriminate movie lover. This is not to say I didn't have my favorite movies and favorite movie stars: Humphrey Bogart, John Garfield, James Cagney, Cary Grant, Edward G. Robinson, Van Johnson, Randolph Scott, Joel McCrea, Errol Flynn, James Stewart and on occasion Burt Lancaster. Later on, of course, I admired Marlon Brando. I absolutely loved Gene Kelly especially in *Singin' in the Rain* (d:Gene Kelly, Stanley Donen,1952). I thought Fred Astaire did his best work in the thirties, when I was too young to appreciate him. In the year I was born, 1933, he made *Flying Down to Rio* (d: Thornton Freeland) in which he and Ginger Rogers appeared together for the first time, dancing to the Academy Award nominated song "Carioca."

Like most young boys, I also had definite reactions to female stars. For example, I never liked Bette Davis or Joan Crawford; they were too neurotic for my taste. I felt that Ava Gardner was too reckless. Betty Grable and June Allyson were too sweet. Lana Turner too dangerous. Rita Hayworth, Hedy Lamarr and Ginger Rogers I considered entirely out of my league. Then there was Teresa Wright. As far as I was concerned she was the best of the lot. This was my kind of girl. There was no mystery about her. She was honest and decent. Most of all, she seemed dependable; someone who wouldn't desert a guy if he got into trouble, or leave him for somebody else. In virtually all of her early roles she always believed the best about the man she loved and was willing to stand by him through thick and thin, as she did when Gary Cooper, portraying the legendary baseball player Lou Gehrig, was struck down at the height of his career with a deadly disease in *The Pride of the Yankees* (d: Sam Wood,1942); or in *Shadow of a Doubt* (d: Alfred Hitchcock,1943) when, in the face of mounting evidence, she refused to believe her Uncle Charlie (Joseph Cotton) was guilty of murder; or with despondent, out-of-work WW II veteran Dana Andrews in *The Best Years of Our Lives* (d: William Wyler,1946); and with Marlon Brando, a WW II veteran, who returns home a paraplegic to face his young wife in *The Men* (d: Fred Zinnemann,1950).

Besides her on-screen persona which highlighted her sincerity and dependability, I also thought she was very attractive. When I was twelve or thirteen I harbored the thought that she would be ten times better to kiss and fool around with than most of the so-called "glamour girls" Hollywood trotted out in those days. As I think about it now, I can see that my youthful infatuation with her was entirely understandable. She possessed the qualities a kid might easily be drawn to to fill the void left by his mother's untimely death. In an uncertain world, she represented an ideal of beauty and dependability. And she was young and healthy enough so that I didn't have to worry about her dying.

I fell in love with Teresa Wright all over again in 1997 when she accepted a small part in *The Rainmaker* (d:Francis

Ford Coppola). I must say I was shocked when she first appeared on screen and I saw how much she had aged over the last half century. What did I expect? I don't know! You see, I had carried this youthful image of her around in my head all those years, and I was crushed to see that she grew old like everybody else. Anyway, I was pleased to see that at seventy-nine, when she made *The Rainmaker*, she still had the same soft, inviting smile, the twinkly eyes, and distinctive voice that had captured my heart years ago. She succumbed to a heart attack in 2004 and died at the age of eighty-six. At the time of her death I remember feeling sad that I had never had the opportunity to tell her how much her performances had meant to me when I was growing up.

One of the movies my sister insisted we see was *A Tree Grows in Brooklyn* (d: Elia Kazan, 1945) starring Peggy Ann Garner, James Dunn and Dorothy McGuire. It was the story of a young girl eager to get an education, while living with her Irish emigrant parents in Brooklyn at the turn of the Twentieth century — all of them struggling to love each other, but with barely enough money for food as well as having the burden of an alcoholic father. Looking back on my sister's choice, I am struck by the similarities between the heroine's determination to get an education that would lift her out of the working class and my sister's own resolve to accomplish the same goal.

Another film I can recall that my sister insisted we see was *The Moon is Blue* (d: Otto Preminger, 1953). It was released the same year *Playboy* magazine made its debut along with the publication of the second *Kinsey Report* that once again, to the horror of much of the general public, challenged conventional beliefs about sexuality. At the time of the film's release, it was considered very racy, telling the story of two aging playboys who attempt to dissuade an attractive young woman from keeping her vow to remain a virgin until her wedding night. A lot of publicity focused on the heretofore taboo use of the word "*virgin*" in the movie. The cast included William Holden, David Niven and Maggie McNamara. I was home on leave from the Navy when we saw this film, which I found tedious. Like *A Tree Grows in Brooklyn*, the subject matter of this film may have held special interest for my sister, who was twenty-three at the time, and like many young women her age she may have been grappling with her own sexuality in those changing times. If you ever want to know what life was like for a teenage Jewish girl growing up under straitened conditions in the Bronx (it could just as easily have been Brooklyn) in the 1940s, read Samuel Freedman's *Who She Was*—an intimate retrospective of his mother's pre-marital life.

It is interesting to note that Betty Friedan, the author, organizer, teacher and driving force behind the women's liberation movement in the 1960s, confessed in her memoir, *Life So Far*, that she regretted having protected her virginity when she was an honors student at Smith College in the 1940s. She said she would get dizzy from all that sexual feeling that she loved, but had resolved not to "go all the way." As an adult, Friedan wasn't against marriage per se, but she was critical of housewives who basked in their husband's glory. For many young women the 1940s and 1950s could have been confusing times to grow up. Women were victims of powerful cultural stereotypes which pressured them to accept systemic male domination.

Debbie Reynolds offered up the popular solution to the female predicament in *The Tender Trap* (1955) when she sang the praises of matrimony. "Honestly, don't you think marriage is the most important thing in the world? I mean, a woman isn't a woman at all until she's married and has had children." This remark (most likely written with tongue in cheek) was part of the "happy Doris Day-like housewife" stereotyping that was going on at the time in movies, TV and magazines and which made Friedan grind her teeth. Her prescription for a fulfilled life for educated housewives was to pursue a career and motherhood at the same time. For Friedan, there was more to life than being a devoted wife and a good mother to her children.

Unfortunately, during the 1940s and '50s, many women were not comfortable in the bedroom and had not yet been accepted in the boardroom. And when it came to sex, a preponderance of women were too diffident to assert themselves. They were either too afraid or too embarrassed to stand up (or lie down) and say—to their boyfriends or husbands—what was on their minds, or to express what they were feeling in their bodies. Although they secretly desired sex, they had to wait until the man made the first move. The complexity of this dynamic was captured brilliantly in the movie *The Egg and I* (d: Chester Erskine, 1947), with Claudette Colbert and Fred Mac Murray appearing as husband and wife. In one scene we see Colbert in bed waiting for Mac Murray to join her. He is off-camera brushing his teeth in the bathroom and insipidly describing to her how he intends for them to spend the rest of their lives together—which includes buying a chicken farm. While he drones on we see Colbert fluffing up the pillow next to her and gently fingering the top of her nightgown, as she responds to his comments. "Whatever my husband decides is all right with me." But it is quite obvious from her facial expressions and sensual body language, and the way she delivers that line, that she's not attempting to be a deferential wife. What she wants at that very moment is sex, and she'll agree to just about anything— even living on a chicken farm—if only he will stop talking and get under the sheets. This scene may have gotten past the Hollywood censors, but it most certainly didn't get past the audience, most of them women.

In many ways my sister was ahead of her time. By 1950 she was attending City College of New York to further her education to help achieve the goal she had set for herself of rising above her working-class background and finding success in the middle class and beyond—a feat she accomplished admirably. Years after her graduation she married (more about this later) and raised two children while pursuing a career. Trained as a statistician, she eventually opened her own CPA practice which she ran until she was eighty-two. It well may be that having experienced our mother's untimely death, she found comfort and security in dealing with numbers because in an accountant's orderly world two plus two will always equal four. There is no room for chance or uncertainty, and if the numbers didn't add up, by God, my sister would figure out why.

As I said above, these were confusing times for a lot of young women who had to deal with changing cultural ideas about marriage, sex and careers, and this included my sister and my ex-wife whom I met in one of my journalism classes at New York University and married in 1958. . . and this is probably as good a time as any to discuss the early years of my marriage. At the time I was young and had no experience living with a woman. I grew up living with my father, a patient, practical, even-tempered person—which, it goes without saying, left me totally unprepared to face the trials and tribulations of marriage—especially to a young woman who had yet to figure out who she was and what she wanted out of life. Unfortunately, the cultural paradigm that existed at the time we met was so powerful that we both unquestioningly accepted the idea that it was time to get married, buy a house in the suburbs, have a car in the garage, raise a family and acquire life insurance. We were expected to follow the norm, which we did, unhappily, in spades.

By the time we met I was desperate to get married, to start a family of my own and create the home life I had never had as a child. This was an emotional imperative for me, and when I met my soon-to-be-wife, I hurried us headlong into marriage. Even though I observed red lights along the way, I ignored all of the warning signals telling me we were not suited for each other. I was like a runaway train hurtling through the darkness and my young, unworldly wife-to-be was programmed to jump on board with me and hold on for dear life.

Whatever doubts she may have had about the benefits of marriage, in general—and specifically to me—she was certain of one thing: she wanted children, or, at least, she thought she did, until they reached the age of seven or eight when they began asserting their independence. Parenting was one thing; bringing children into the world was an entirely different matter. Luckily for her we were both very fertile, so that the necessary business of begetting offspring was kept to a minimum. To be perfectly honest about this act of procreation, it felt (to me, anyway) more like participating in an experiment in a high school biology class than a labor of love.

Except for the first year of our marriage, my ex-wife was a stay-at-home-wife. Like many other women in our suburban neighborhood in New Rochelle (where we moved when Julie and Tracy were quite young) she volunteered her services with the PTA, the Brownies and other community-affiliated projects. To this day I don't know what in her mind made it possible for her to endure a loveless and sexually arid marriage for over twenty years. The only thing I can think of, is that she was reluctant to give up a financially comfortable lifestyle with very few, if any, demands made on her by me. For my part, I suffered this ordeal because I felt a responsibility toward my daughters, to be a presence in their lives until they were old enough (or almost old enough) to go out into the world on their own. Fortunately, I had my own business which was thriving, and I channeled most of my energies into it. What pleasure and satisfaction I didn't receive at home from my wife I received from my daughters and my work which was enough for me at the time.

I realized (that is, I *fully* realized) that my marriage was not destined to flourish by our second or third wedding anniversary.

I remember stopping in a Hallmark store on my way home from work to buy my wife an anniversary card. I must have read through every anniversary greeting card in the store and could not find a single one that honestly conveyed my feelings. Almost all of them had sentimental messages about the joys of matrimony and love everlasting, and I could not bring myself to purchase any of them because it would have been an outright lie. What I was looking for was an anniversary card that expressed despondency and hopelessness, but Hallmark doesn't make anniversary cards like that. After forty-five minutes of fruitless searching, I walked out of the store without buying a card, and I never purchased one in the years that followed. I felt it was hard enough living a lie, without my having to celebrate it.

It must have been early on in our marriage that my wife realized she wasn't cut out for the life I offered her, the wife of a corporate businessman. She increasingly balked at accompanying me to social functions with business associates and their wives— either at their homes or ours—even if the occasion included dinner at an up-scale restaurant in Manhattan followed by a Broadway show. Were my feelings hurt by her coolness? Yes. Was I disappointed that my marriage was not turning out the way I had envisioned? Yes. Was I angry? Only in the beginning. Over time I came to accept the idea that the life we shared was not the life either one of us wanted, and I knew that blaming her would be hurtful and wouldn't change anything. At such times being quiet speaks volumes.

When two people get divorced (as we eventually did) it is not easy to say who was right and who was wrong, as one of my favorite stories makes clear.

At the beginning of the last century on the Lower East Side, rabbis often lived in the same buildings as their congregates; and since there were no psychiatrists in those days, if one of the members had a problem he or she would go to the rabbi for advice. So one evening there was a knock on the door of a rabbi's apartment. His wife answered the door. It was Mr. Grossman from 4A. He asked if he could see the rabbi. Certainly, she said, and showed him into the living room. As the men began to talk, she walked back to the kitchen and listened to their conversation behind a curtain.

"What's the trouble?", the rabbi asked?

"It's my wife," said Mr. Grossman. " I want a divorce."

"What's so terrible you need a divorce?" asked the rabbi.

"What's so terrible? You ask! She's the worst house cleaner in the world, and the worst cook, too. When I come home at night from work she never asks me how I feel, or what happened at work. Instead, she starts complaining to me about her troubles. This hurts and that hurts, and she doesn't have enough money to buy food or clothes for the children. And one thing more. Her mother comes to visit us three times a week and she hasn't said a word to me since the day we got married. So that's it. I'm finished. Done. I want a divorce."

The rabbi thought for a minute and then said to Grossman, "You know something, you're right. You're absolutely right." Mr. Grossman thanked the rabbi and left.

The next night Mrs. Grossman knocked at the door and asked to see the rabbi. The rabbi's wife showed her in and then, like the previous night, stood behind the kitchen curtain and listened in.

"So what can I do for you Mrs. Grossman," the rabbi asked.

"What you can do for me is give me a divorce. I've been married to my husband for ten years and I can't take it anymore."

" What seems to be the trouble?, asked the rabbi.

" I'll tell you what the trouble is. He never puts anything away. He leaves his dirty clothes on the floor where he takes them off. He can't stand my mother. He's got bad breath, and whenever we sit down to a meal he reads the newspaper and ignores me. And in bed he has gas. It's terrible. What kind of life is this? I've had enough. I want a divorce."

The rabbi paused momentarily and said, "You know something, Mrs. Grossman? You're right. You're absolutely right."

Mrs. Grossman thanked the rabbi and left. No sooner was she out the door than the rabbi's wife came storming into the living room. "How could you do such a thing," she said. "Last night you told Mr. Grossman he was right, and tonight you told Mrs. Grossman she was right. They both can't be right."

After a moment's thought the rabbi said to his wife, "You know something? You're right, you're absolutely right."

Chapter Seventeen

Now then, back to my adolescent years in the Bronx.

When we moved to the Bronx my father enrolled me in P.S. 16 on Carpenter Avenue, about twelve blocks from our apartment house. One morning my father drove me to school and introduced me to the principal, Mr. Greenberg, a pleasant but stern administrator who struck fear in the heart of any child caught in the hallways without a pass. After a few private words with him, my father left me in his care and went off to work. Upon his departure Mr. Greenberg put his arm around my shoulder and walked me to my first classroom where I was introduced to the art teacher, Mrs. Heller. She was an attractive, middle-aged, motherly-type woman with beautiful soft gray hair. She was wearing a colorful smock imprinted with large flowers which I thought suited her role. I liked her the minute I saw her. In some ways she reminded me of Mrs. Cohen. I remember standing next to Mr. Greenberg at the front of the classroom. All the kids in their seats stopped whatever it was they were doing and looked up at me. Mr. Greenberg left me standing by myself for a moment as he walked over to Mrs. Heller and spoke to her. Although I couldn't hear what he was saying, I had the feeling he was talking about me and explaining the details of my home life. When Mr. Greenberg returned to my side he once more placed his arm around my shoulder, only this time it felt like a lead weight and made me feel terribly self-conscious. As we stood there, side-by-side facing the class, he said, " I want you all to meet Stephen Zimmerman. He's a new student here at our school and I hope you will make him feel welcome."

I remember very clearly that at P.S. 16 there was something called "Mother's Day." This was a day set aside for mothers to come to school to visit with their child's teachers to discuss his or her progress. Several days before this event occurred, my home-room teacher, Mrs. Flynn, passed out a mimeographed notice for students to take home to remind their mothers to come to school on the appointed date. Most of the kids stuffed these notices in their notebooks to take home. I quickly placed mine in my pants pocket. On the way home from school that afternoon, walking along Richardson Avenue, about two blocks from my apartment house, I removed the piece of paper from my pocket and read it. Sure enough, right at the top it said, "Mother's Day." For a moment I felt as though I was going to cry, but I didn't. I just crumpled up the notice and threw it angrily in the gutter.

I think being surrounded (in our new apartment) by the familiar furniture from my parents' old apartment on Andrews Avenue, had a disturbing effect on my psyche. Whatever it was—my parents' bed (that I now slept in with my father, and did so until I left home to join the Navy— not an uncommon practice at a time when children often shared beds with parents or siblings). Maybe it was the furniture or drapes, or the paintings, the dishes, silverware or bathroom towels. Whatever it was, it seemed to stir up memories of my mother.

With them came a recurrent nightmare that I experienced several times a year until I was about sixteen—a nightmare that is etched in my memory, and that up until now I have never shared with anyone. In this terrifying dream I would hear my mother cry out for help. Her plaintive voice would come from a primeval forest that drew me into its darkness. Following the sound of my mother's voice, I would run toward her as fast as I could, sensing that her life was in danger. Shortly thereafter I would come upon a clearing in the forest, and here I could see my mother before me, trapped in quicksand only several yards away from where I was standing. The thick mud was already up to her chin as she continued to call out for help—not to me personally, but to anyone who might be able to offer assistance. I thought it strange there was no sense of panic in her voice nor any sign of fear on her face—only a pathetic expression of resignation as though she were asking for help she knew in her heart would not be forthcoming. Just when I decided to attempt to reach out and grab hold of her, a tall, black, spiked iron fence shot up before me to block my efforts. I found it impossible to squeeze between the bars to reach her, nor could I climb over the fence. I quickly realized the helplessness of my situation. There was nothing I could do except stand there, impotently, holding tightly onto the iron bars and watch my mother's head slowly sink beneath the viscous sea of mud.

At this point the dream would end. Each nightmare was the same in every detail, and its disturbing effects made it difficult for me to go back to sleep that night or for several nights after.

What follows are a few snapshot memories from this period of my life that reveal something about how, in small ways, my father and I attempted to look out for each other:

For the life of me I cannot recall how or where we did our laundry. However, I do recall folding our newly-washed clothes on the kitchen table. I also remember placing a towel on the table to use as an ironing board. The only two items I remember ironing were our white T-shirts, and my father's white handkerchiefs. It was important to me that his handkerchiefs were ironed so that when he removed one in public from his back pocket everyone would think he came from a clean, respectable home . . . not from one that was rarely, if ever, dusted (which is why I never invited any of my friends home). I also remember that during the winter months my socks would be stiff as a board. In the morning, on those infrequent occasions when I bothered to put on a clean pair, my father would place them for a few minutes on the hissing radiator in the living room and then rub them between his hands to soften them up for me so they would be comfortable to wear.

Many evenings my father would come home with both arms full of shopping bags from A&P on 241st. Street. Instead of offering to relieve him of one of the bags (why I didn't think of this I don't know!), I followed him into the lobby of our apartment house. As he began to climb the stairs I would place my head under his butt and push his weary body up the stairs to our apartment.

One day I was sick with a sore throat and stuffy nose that was bad enough to keep me home from school. Before he left for work, my father brought the radio into the bedroom from the kitchen and placed it on the night table next to the bed. On a piece of paper he wrote down the times I was supposed to take my cough syrup. Then he left the house. But he returned ten minutes later. He had gone downstairs to the candy store and bought me ten different comic books so that I wouldn't get bored or lonely. Between coughing, sneezing, blowing my nose, reading my comics and taking naps, I managed to get through the day. I don't remember what I did for lunch. Maybe I made myself a peanut butter and jelly sandwich or warmed up a can of Dinty Moore Beef Stew. The worst part of the day was around 4 o'clock when gray, wintry shadows began to cast the apartment in darkness, and it was too early for my favorite radio programs to come on the air; but when they did, my imagination came alive. Every character, every piece of action—a car door slamming, a punch to the jaw, footsteps up a dark, creaky staircase—played out inside my head and gripped my attention. Beginning at 5:15 I could listen to The Adventures of Superman broadcast over WOR, followed by Capt. Midnight at five-thirty on the same station, or I could change stations to WJZ and listen to Jack Armstrong "The All-American Boy." The last program of the afternoon I usually listened to began at 5:45. It was the Tom Mix show which took place in "Dobie Township" on the "T.M. Bar Ranch" with Tom Mix , his horse "Tony," and his friends and cohorts, everyone one of them "Straight Shooters." Around the time the show ended my father would walk through the front door and start to get dinner ready.

*   *   *

Along with radio shows and movie stars, I also had my favorite comic book heroes. The American comic book, as we know it, came into existence in New York City as an inexpensive way to capitalize on the success that newspaper comic strips had achieved. This was accomplished by turning out a number of comic books featuring superhuman heroes whose instant popularity helped turn comic books into a major industry reaching its peak during the late 1930s through the late 1940s—which pretty much coincided with the golden age of radio, Big Band music and Hollywood movies. Many of the comic book creators—the artists, writers, editors and publishers—came from Jewish immigrant families living on the Lower East Side and its environs. Like the Jewish movie moguls before them, these entrepreneurs managed to get in on the ground floor of a new industry before there were any racial barriers, written or otherwise, that might have impeded their development —like advertising agencies who refused employment, as a general policy, to Jews and other "ethnics" (i.e. Italians or Irish Catholics)—a ban not lifted until the mid-1960s.

During its heyday as a mainstream art form, there were comic book heroes of virtually every stripe: Hawkman, Sandman, Johnny Thunder, the Green Lantern, and the Flash, who wore Mercury's helmet (which looked like a shallow soup bowl turned upside down) with a pair of wings sticking out on both sides giving him the ability to move with the speed of light. Plastic Man, another favorite of mine, was able to stretch his neck and arms around corners and peek through open windows on the top floor of skyscrapers. He acquired this supernatural ability by accident when in his previous life as a gangster a certain chemical entered his body through an open wound. Fortunately for all of us this accident also transformed his nature from that of a villain to that of a public defender of justice.

Superman, the "Man of Steel," made his debut in 1938 in *Action Comics* and was high on my reading list, as it was with just about every kid at that time who was old enough to read. Of course, the Batman character was also at the top of my list. He made his first appearance in *Detective Comics* less than a year after the appearance of Superman. He became so popular that "Batman" became a self-titled comic book series that began publishing under the Batman name in 1940, at which time his sidekick, Robin, "The Boy Wonder," was introduced to fans and the moniker "Dynamic Duo" was forevermore enshrined in comic book history. In real life, Batman was billionaire philanthropist Bruce Wayne who, as a small child, witnessed his parents' murder during a mugging in Gotham City, a fictional municipality overrun with crime, graft and corruption. He was so traumatized by the event that when he grew up he devoted his life to waging war on crime, transforming his boyhood fear into a determination to break up crime rings.

Red Ryder and his youthful companion Little Beaver were my favorite western heroes. Red Ryder always wore a bright red shirt and the letter "R" printed on his chaps. I thought it was great how the creators of the strip made Little Beaver speak "Indian talk." "If me no do something him catch-um me." When Captain Marvel hit the newsstands in February, 1940, in WHIZ comics, he quickly became my new favorite hero. In real life,

Captain Marvel was Billy Matson, a teenager who worked as a radio news reporter for station WHIZ. Billy acquired his extraordinary powers from an ancient wizard named Shazam. Whenever Billy utters the old man's name he is immediately struck by a lightning bolt (a yellow symbol emblazoned on his costume) and is instantly transformed into a red-clad giant of a man, "The World's Mightiest Mortal." One of the characters I liked best in these stories was Captain Marvel's arch nemesis, a crazy, bald-headed scientist named Dr. Sivana who had this snickering laugh, "Heh! Heh! Heh!" I remember that Dr. Sivana derisively nicknamed Captain Marvel "The Big Red Cheese." At the height of its popularity Captain Marvel sold about 1.4 million copies per issue making it the most widely circulated comic book in America at the time.

It wasn't long before a couple of heroines came thundering onto the scene, namely Sheena, Queen of the Jungle, followed by Wonder Woman, Princess of the Amazon. Sheena, the female version of Tarzan, was either an orphan or had been abandoned and, like Tarzan, learned to communicate with animals in order to survive. She made her debut in 1938, and in 1942 she became the first female comic character with her own title. I was captivated by her. Here was this gorgeous blonde, wearing a skimpy leopard skin outfit, with dangling earrings, rushing through the jungle mostly in pursuit of white explorers intent on stealing animals and valuable relics from her savage kingdom. Bob Powell, one of several artists who drew this strip, really knew how to show off her best features without being lewd. At twelve years old, this was the closest thing I'd come in contact with that could possibly be classified as pornographic. I envied her "handsome consort" Bob who, as I remember, followed her around the jungle, at times getting himself into trouble and needing to be rescued by her.

With the beginning of World War II a host of new superheroes was created—not to fight gangsters and petty thieves—but to wage war on foreign saboteurs and other criminal elements out to destroy all that was good and decent in America. My all-time favorite was Captain America. He was the alter ego of Steve Rogers, a frail young man whose strength was brought to near human perfection by an experimental serum in order to aid the United States in its fight against the Axis powers. On the front cover of one of the comic books I read at the time, it showed Captain America punching Adolf Hitler in the jaw. His most reliable weapon was an indestructible red, white, and blue shield that he could also throw to fell his enemies, sometimes at buck-toothed caricatures of Japanese soldiers.

I remember years later that I recreated my father's act of "comic book" kindness when my daughter, Tracy, about seven or eight years old was home from school with a sore throat and stuffy nose. When I returned home from work that night I presented her with ten of her favorite comic books. I think I did this as much for myself as I did for Tracy because I saw it as an opportunity to recapture a cherished moment from my past, and at the same time to pass along my father's thoughtfulness to one of my children.

Chapter Eighteen

During the school year, before my father left for work, he would always leave a one-dollar bill on the kitchen table. The dollar was for my lunch and a snack after school. Later on, when I began attending high school in Manhattan, he placed two pennies next to the dollar bill so I could purchase the Daily News every morning before I got on the elevated train into the city. He knew I loved to read the sports pages that reported the previous day's performance of the Brooklyn Dodgers and NY Yankees, complete with box scores.

In the opinion of many sports writers and journalists, the 1940s was one of the greatest decades in the history of baseball. According to Hal Bodley, the dean of American baseball writers, "No one has yet figured out exactly when baseball was invented, but the modern game we know and love today was forged in the crucible of the 1940s." More than ever, baseball was considered as American as apple pie. It was America's game. It was the people's game. It defined us as a nation. Rooting for your favorite baseball team—in New York it was either the Yankees, Giants or Brooklyn Dodgers—was taken as seriously as one's religion. Almost every kid in the Bronx knew Joe DiMaggio's batting average and how many hits he had gotten the day before. And if you lived in Brooklyn, or were a secret Dodgers fan as I was, you knew the same stats about Jackie Robinson. Men attended games in suits, shirts, ties, and fedoras and those sitting in sun-drenched bleachers would mop their perspiring necks and brows with white handkerchiefs. And at the end of each game, ballplayers would leave the park and head home to Queens, Brooklyn, or the Bronx on the subway, sitting down right next to their most loyal fans—mostly blue-collar "stiffs" returning home from work.

Not even the disruption of World War II could diminish baseball's importance and popularity. Approximately one month after the attack on Pearl Harbor, baseball Commissioner Kenesaw Mountain Landis asked President Roosevelt whether he should cancel baseball or keep the game going. Roosevelt told him that baseball was critically important to the American people, and that the game should go on to help sustain the people's moral on the home front. By the beginning of 1944, nearly sixty percent of the major league ballplayers had traded in their baseball uniforms for the uniform of the armed services.

With so many players serving in the armed forces, major league teams were desperate to find suitable replacements, which led the Cincinnati Reds to hire a 15-year-old high school pitching phenom, Joe Nuxhall, who pitched only one game in 1945 and got knocked around, but years later returned to the major leagues and had a successful career. The Brooklyn Dodgers, looking to replace Pee Wee Reese at shortstop, hired sixteen-year-old Brooklyn native, Tommy Brown, who played in 46 games in 1944 and hit .164. Not to be outdone, the St Louis Browns hired Pete Gray, a one-armed outfielder who played in 77 games in 1945 and hit .218.

So many historic and zany events occurred in baseball during this decade, that it has become etched in the minds of ardent baseball fans for all eternity. For example, between May 15 and July 16, 1941, Joe DiMaggio, the "Yankee Clipper," hit safely in 56 consecutive games— an incredible feat that still stands to this day. During the 1940s, the New York Yankees faced their cross-town rivals, the Brooklyn Dodgers, in three World Series (1941, 1947 and 1949) defeating the Dodgers on all three occasions. The Dodgers had to wait until 1955 before they beat the Yankees in seven games, capturing the team's first World Series championship .

Then there was Ted Williams,the Boston Red Sox icon, who ended the 1941 season hitting over .400. On the final day of the season his average was .3995, and probably would have been rounded up to .400 in the record books. His teammates and manager urged him to sit out the last day of the season to protect his historic batting average. But Williams would have none of it. He insisted on playing even though there was a chance that his batting average could drop below the .400 mark and ruin his chance for immortality. It was a doubleheader day against the Philadelphia A's, and, as it turned out, Williams played both games and went 6-for-8, finishing the season with a .406 batting average — the last player to hit .400 or better during a single season.

During this momentous decade, while the New York Yankees

piled on victory after victory in the American League, the St. Louis Cardinals won four National League pennants and three World Series, making them the last NL team to play in three consecutive World Series (1942-1944). Leading the charge for the Cardinals was Stan "The Man" Musial whose prodigious hitting power put him in a class by himself, hitting over .300 year after year.

In 1947 television began its monumental impact on baseball when all sixteen teams, with the exception of the Pittsburgh Pirates, negotiated local TV deals to broadcast home games.

Perhaps the most significant event of the decade took place on April 15, 1947, when Jackie Robinson put an end to institutionalized bigotry when he played his first game for the Brooklyn Dodgers. Bill Veeck, owner of the Cleveland Indians, signed Larry Doby on July 5, 1947, making him the first black player in the American League. At the end of their careers, both players were inducted into baseball's Hall of Fame.

The Brooklyn Dodgers became an infinitely better baseball team after Jackie Robinson joined the club. I was enthralled by his consistent hitting for extra bases, but mostly by his base-running and base-stealing exploits, especially when he attempted to steal home, an almost unprecedented feat at the time. Robinson would dance wildly up and down the third base line distracting the pitcher and generally driving him crazy. And then when the pitcher, standing on the mound with the ball in his hand, momentarily turned his gaze away from third base, Robinson would—when he thought the timing was just right—make a mad dash to steal home, usually arriving safely under the catcher's tag. Robinson hit .297 that year and walked away with the

Rookie of the Year Award, helping the Dodgers capture the National League pennant. He also won my admiration and loyalty because I sensed the importance of what he stood for and what he was attempting to achieve. What better hero to have in American history, I thought, than a baseball player.

My veneration of Jackie Robinson was shared by millions of baseball fans, none more fervently than President Jimmy Carter's mother, Lillian, who considered it to be one of God's special blessings that she and her husband, Earl, were present when Jackie Robinson played his first game for the Brooklyn Dodgers in 1947. During the period when her son occupied the White House, she would telephone manager Tommy Lasorda from time to time to offer advice and challenge some of his managerial decisions. She remained an ardent Dodgers fan till the day she died, even after the ball club moved to Los Angeles in 1958 and the Braves moved to Atlanta in 1966.

In my opinion Barack Obama, the first African-American President in the history of the United States, was the Jackie Robinson of politics. No matter how many death threats (like the ones Robinson received), or racial slurs were hurled at him, directly or indirectly, he never took the bait; he never dropped his bat and rushed the mound to pummel the offender. He played the game fair and square—as best one can on an uneven political playing field—never resorting to unsportsmanlike conduct. He, too, is my hero.

Because I had lived with Aunt Lee immediately after my mother died, and for a few years off and on after that, I had early on become a devoted Brooklyn Dodgers fan. This proved to be a bit nerve-wracking when my father and I moved to the Bronx, because almost every one of my new friends was a Yankees fan. To me the Yankees were vapid. They always played by the book and lacked the spark and spontaneity that characterized the Brooklyn Dodgers and made them so exciting to watch—or to listen to on the radio with the play-by-play action being described by "Red" Barber, "The Ol' Redhead," in the folksy Southern style that made him an institution in Brooklyn during the 1940s, before he defected to the Yankees in 1954. Even Tallulah Bankhead, the outspoken Broadway and Hollywood actress and avid baseball fan, remarked "The Yankees bored the bloomers off of me." On the other hand, with the Dodgers, something unexpected could always happen on the field, and something usually did.

Caught in a quandary, I remained a closeted Brooklyn Dodger fan all through my teenage years in fear of being "outed" and running the risk of ostracism, or, worse, having to fight to defend my ball-playing heroes—"The Brooklyn Bums." The truth is, when it came to fistfights I lacked an appetite for inflicting pain on others, although my opponents, usually much bigger than me, didn't have too much to fear. In the few fistfights I did have as a kid, I had an outstandingly poor record. Most fights consisted in wrestling someone to the ground with maybe one or two punches being thrown. Fights usually ended with one of the combatants sitting on the chest of his opponent, and pinning to the ground his outstretched arms above his head, demanding that his victim say "Uncle" or "Give," to signal his surrender. On those few occasions when I did get into a fight and lost, I never felt ashamed. Somehow I always knew from a very early age that manhood was measured by a different form of valor.

My recollection of fistfights would not be complete if I

didn't, once again, jump ahead in time to describe one fight I did have. It took place not when I was a kid, but when I was a young man serving in the Navy.

Our ship was anchored off the coast of Cuba. For want of something better to do on a bright Sunday afternoon, my fellow shipmates thought a good way to pass the time would be to arrange a series of boxing matches so they could watch guys beat the crap out of each other. While I didn't think this was a particularly great way to spend an afternoon, I didn't feel I was in a position to argue against this macho form of entertainment. As it turned out, I was purposely and unevenly matched with a tall, muscular, good ol' farm boy from down south who was as dumb as a box of rocks. The matchmakers thought it would be great sport to watch the little Jew bastard from New York get his brains beat out by this towering, slow-moving oaf. And they were right about one thing: if he ever had connected with a right to my jaw, I would have been picked up by a cop for speeding. As soon as we put the boxing gloves on, I started circling the great beast. I would bob and weave in and out, trying to stay out of harm's way. I was like a pesky fly buzzing around an elephant. To keep this Goliath at bay I would occasionally dart inside and pepper him with a few left jabs to his midsection. The thought of attempting to reach up and take a swing at his jaw seemed like a ridiculous idea, and could have left me open to a wild right hook or uppercut. As I danced, he continued to swing wildly hoping to connect with one good punch to my head. But I was too fast for him. By the time the three minutes were up my legs were a little wobbly, but otherwise I was unhurt. I was just glad to get out of there with my head still attached to my shoulders.

Chapter Nineteen

Under our apartment house was a small grocery store operated by the Anderson sisters, two spinsters who lived in our building. They opened early in the morning and stayed open late at night to serve their customers. Today we would think of them as a convenience store operating in the shadows of the large A&P supermarket three blocks away. Food items, almost entirely canned goods and boxes of foodstuffs, were stacked on shelves that reached almost up to the ceiling. The sisters had to use a long pole with metal claws at the end to retrieve the products stored on the topmost shelves. Ritchie Schultz, a tall, muscular kid living with his mother in our building, worked for the Anderson sisters after school stocking and restocking the shelves for them.

Right next store was a candy store owned by Mr. and Mrs. Lapinsky. I always felt that Mrs. Lapinsky looked after me in a special way. Whenever I ordered a milkshake I noticed she made me a larger serving than she made for other kids. She would watch to make sure I finished every last drop. "Finish it," she would say, "It's good for you. Make you grow up strong."

Next to the candy store was Lee's Chinese hand laundry. Every once in a while, as a childish prank, several of my friends and I would run past Mr. Lee's open door and yell at him, "No tickee, no washee." Something inside of me told me this wasn't the right thing to do, but I did it anyway to show I was one of the guys. Mr. Lee would respond to our taunts by rushing to the front door in his slippers and shaking his iron at us as we ran away.

At the age of twelve or thirteen I had not yet read Ralph Waldo Emerson's *Self-Reliance* which sets out the argument for keeping one's own counsel while resisting peer pressure and remaining true to one's inner voice.

> What I must do is all that concerns me, not what the people think. This rule, equally arduous in actual and in intellectual life, may serve for the whole distinction between greatness and meanness. It is the harder, because you will always find those who think they know what is your duty better than you know it. It is easy in the world to live after the world's opinion; it is easy in solitude to live after our own; but the great man is he who in the midst of the crowd keeps with perfect sweetness the independence of solitude.

A few doors down from the Chinese Laundry was Patsy's barbershop. Patsy, an Italian immigrant, was a slightly built man in his mid-forties who enjoyed yakking with his customers in broken English. In the front of the store he would cut hair. In the back of the store he practiced his violin and operated an amateur short-wave radio. I believe every kid in our building got his hair cut by Patsy. And it didn't make much difference how you combed your hair, or whether you had straight or wavy hair, or what shape your head was; every kid got pretty much the same cut. After your haircut Patsy would pour some gunk on your head from a fancy green bottle, and for the next several days your hair looked like it had been coated with shellac, and remained this way until the next time you took a bath, which was usually once a week. Once in a while a kid would get his hair cut and when he returned to his apartment to show his mother she might not like the way it looked. If she didn't, she'd bring her kid back to Patsy's and insist he fix it. Naturally, the kid was humiliated, especially if his friends were in the shop looking on. In these instances the kid's mother would stand right next to Patsy showing him where to cut off a little here, a little there, then straighten it a little here, until she was satisfied her son had gotten a "good haircut" this time.

Located at the back of our apartment house was a court-yard and a large storeroom where families stored baby carriages, bicycles, tricycles, beach chairs and other bulky items that took up too much space in people's apartments. There was a slight inclined ramp leading out of the courtyard which mothers used to wheel or carry their belongings up to the street level. The janitor used it to wheel garbage cans up to the curb. On occa-sional Sunday mornings a middle-aged man, attired in a shabby-looking suit, stood in the center of the courtyard and serenaded the tenants with his violin. Several of them, leaning on their windowsills listening to his rhapsodic music, wrapped up a few pennies in small pieces of newspaper and tossed them down to the itinerant musician trying to earn a living. My father always allowed me to do the tossing.

During the time I attended P.S. 16, my breakfast, almost every morning, was a bowl of Kellogg's Pep. Besides the fact that I liked the taste, and it was easy to fix, each package contained a small pin with a colorful picture of one of the characters from the Daily News Sunday comics section, usually referred to as the "funny papers." My collection included The Gumps, Harold Teen, Dick Tracy, Gasoline Alley, Moon Mullins, Smilin' Jack, Smokey Stover, Little Lulu, Orphan Annie, Joe Palooka, Mutt and Jeff, Blondie, and others I can no longer recall.

For lunch I used to visit a small Italian mom-and-pop grocery store right next to P.S. 16. I would get either a ham and cheese sandwich on a seeded roll, or maybe an Italian meatball "Hero" sandwich. Sometimes I would walk up to White Plains Road to a restaurant run by a Greek family and order soup and a hamburger, or a tuna fish or chicken salad sandwich. Most of the kids in my class either went home for lunch or brought it with them in a brown bag. On meatless Fridays, many of the Italian kids brought a sandwich of scrambled eggs and green peppers which they stored on the top shelf in the clothes closet where the heating ducts were located. During the winter months, when the doors were rolled open at lunchtime, an odious smell wafted out. To this day I can't stand the smell or taste of green peppers.

When it came to food, living with my father was not like living with Mrs. Cohen. As far as I can remember he never made any special sauces or gravies for dinner, but the simple food he prepared tasted good, and we remained healthy. As a matter of fact, I can remember only one day that my father wasn't feeling well, so I didn't go to high school that day. Instead, I drove him around in his truck picking up and delivering tires to his customers, all of whom, I discovered, called him "Zimmy." I don't know what my father did for breakfast; maybe he stopped somewhere for a cup of coffee and a doughnut, or just waited until it was time for lunch when he would stop at a roadside diner. He told me you could always tell if a diner had a good reputation by the number of trucks parked outside.

For dinner my father cooked, no matter how tired he was. I have an indelible image of him peeling potatoes at the kitchen sink with one elbow resting heavily on the white porcelain rim. He usually made mashed potatoes or rice for dinner which he often served with a Del Monte canned vegetable and either hamburgers or a T-bone steak. I'm sure he prepared other foods for dinner, I just can't recall them. I do remember that fish was never on the menu, except occasionally on Sunday mornings when he would broil some chubs (white fish)—for just a minute or two to release the juices—and serve them with bagels and cream cheese, all of which he purchased at Weiner's Dairy directly across the street from our apartment house. During the summer months, when it was still light at 7 p.m., and I was still playing in the street with my friends, my father would lean out of the kitchen window and yell "Stephen." This was my call to dinner. As soon as I heard his voice I would immediately stop whatever game I was involved in and head upstairs. "I gotta go," I would tell my friends.

On Sunday afternoons, if we didn't meet my sister in Manhattan, my father would usually roast a chicken in a large dark blue roasting pan with tiny irregular white specks baked into the shiny enamel that gave it the appearance of a thousand stars set against a night sky. How he learned to cook remains a mystery to me. Once in a while, if he got home from work early, we would take the "A" trolley, which stopped right in front of our apartment house, to Mt. Vernon for a Chinese dinner. (In 1948 buses began replacing trolleys in the Bronx much to my dismay.) On some of these evenings, after dinner, we would take in a movie at RKO Proctor's on Gramatan Avenue. Wednesday nights were special because, in addition to two movies, the theater featured "live" amateur performances showcasing local talent, mostly singers, piano players, a few ventriloquists, and a lot of tap dancers, all with aspirations (mostly delusions) of making it big in show business.

On one particular night the theater was quite crowded and my father and I, along with a number of other people, had to stand at the back of the theater until amateur night was over when many of the patrons who had arrived earlier would get up to leave. My father and I were part of the "standing room only" crowd. Occasionally people milling around us would jostle and elbow each other to get a better view of the stage. At some point a man, considerably taller and younger than my father (who was about sixty-two at the time), got into a shoving match with my father, and before I knew what was happening I heard my father say, "You're not going to shove me, buster." And then the man shouted something back at which point my father angrily responded, "Okay, let's take this outside and settle it." After this retort the argument subsided and my father and I continued to watch the end of amateur night without further incident and, I might add, with an unobstructed view of the stage.

When we returned home from one of these nights out, or from a baseball game at the Polo Grounds, we were usually greeted with a performance of another kind taking place in the kitchen sink. As soon as we turned on the kitchen light we became aware of a regiment of cockroaches scurrying about on night patrol. The light would take them by surprise and they would immediately skitter for cover in an attempt to escape with their lives. Armed with my father's newspaper, and scalding hot water from the faucet, I tried to either beat them to death, or burn them alive, and then wash them down the drain where they probably came from in the first place. I showed no mercy toward my enemy. It was a war that had to be won.

Once again I feel the need to break off the narrative to briefly describe one of those nights when my father took me to the Polo Grounds to watch a game between the New York Giants and the Brooklyn Dodgers—two teams involved in one of the most competitive rivalries in baseball history. I don't remember the score, and I don't remember who won. What I do remember was that the score was tied in the ninth sending the game into extra innings. By this time it was almost eleven o'clock. I turned to my father and said, "We better leave. It's getting late and you have to get up and go to work in the morning." My father, knowing I was a rabid Dodgers fan, said, "No. We've stayed this long we'll stay to the end to see who wins." And we did, and we got home close to one in the morning. My father got up at his usual time and left for work. Shortly after him, I left our apartment to go to school.

On most evenings during and after dinner we would sit at the kitchen table and listen to our favorite programs on our small Emerson radio, the very same radio my father listened to when my mother was alive. I remember at 7:15 there was a fifteen-minute show starring Jack Smith who'd sing and play the piano. I thought he was kind of corny, but you could tell he was trying hard to be a star. On other nights we might listen to *Beulah* (starring Hattie McDaniel in later episodes). After dinner on most nights my father was too tired to get up immediately and do the dishes, so we just sat there in silence, listening to one show after the other, until his energy returned and he got up to clear the table and wash the dishes. One of our favorite programs was the *Lone Ranger* at 7:30 on WJZ. Later in the evening, mostly during the winter months when it was dark and cold outside, we would tune in to *Inner Sanctum,* which always began with the sound of a squeaking door and the ominous chords from an organ, followed by the voice of Raymond Edward Johnson, the show's host. After his ghoulish greeting, Raymond would tell two or three morbid jokes: "If you're looking for a job, he intoned one evening, "there's a good opening in the graveyard—not much pay, but with tomb and board." Other shows we regularly listened to included *Burns and Allen, Arthur Godfrey Talent Scouts, Gangbusters, It Pays to Be Ignorant, Duffy's Tavern, The Green Hornet* and *Amos and Andy* (which throughout its history was often criticized for racial stereotyping but which my father and I took good-naturedly, thoroughly enjoying its engaging characters: Amos, Andy, Kingfish and Madam Queen), *The Shadow,* and the *Red Skelton Show.* One of my very favorite shows was *The Life of Riley* starring William Bendix.

I liked it when Riley got himself in a difficult situation. When this happened he would say, in an exasperated tone, "What a revoltin' development this is." I thought it was funny, too, that his best friend was an undertaker by the name of Digby O'Dell whom Riley always called Digger O'Dell. It's understandable, with this line-up of entertainment, and with no one checking up on me, why I didn't get much, if any, home work done in the evenings. Without his saying so, I felt that my father cherished these evenings as much as I did.

Chapter Twenty

During the 1940s radio was still an important part of most people's lives, and sporting events, mostly baseball games and World Championship boxing matches, were among the most popular with sports fans. One of the most electrifying moments in radio sports history took place on the evening of June 25, 1948. This was the night that champion Joe Louis met "Jersey Joe" Wolcott in a re-match at Yankee Stadium for the world heavyweight title. Both men had faced each other in a fierce battle six months earlier, on December 5, 1947, at Madison Square Garden. Louis narrowly won that fight and agreed to a re-match.

On the night of the fight I vividly recall standing on the sidewalk in front of my apartment building along with about ten other kids and a few grownups. My father was upstairs reading his evening newspaper and sipping a glass of Tudor beer. I don't remember exactly how it came about, but I do remember a group of us forming a huddle under Mr. Kirshner's apartment which was located on the ground floor. This happened at about 10 p.m. when Mr. Kirshner, who had a reputation in our building for "having money," opened his living room window and pulled up his venetian blinds to cool off his apartment as he got ready to listen to the fight which was being broadcast on WJZ. He set a chair next to the window where he had perched his small radio. When a bunch of us started to mill around beneath his window to listen in, he turned the volume way up so we could hear every word of Don Dumphy's blow-by-blow description. We were definitely a partisan crowd, with just about everybody in Louis' corner. In those days when you listened to the radio, especially the fights, you didn't say much except between rounds when a listener or two offered a quick appraisal of who they thought was winning and why. Occasionally you'd find yourself staring blankly at someone's face without the slightest bit of self-consciousness, and them staring right back at you while you both listened silently, intently, to the commentator's words coming out of a small plastic or wooden box.

In the early rounds it wasn't going well for Louis, the "Brown Bomber." Walcott was all business. He had knocked Louis to the canvas in the third round with a hard right to the jaw, and then staggered Louis again in the fifth round with a series of damaging blows to the head and body. Rounds six through nine seemed to belong to a determined Louis, flat-footedly pursuing Walcott who kept dancing and sidestepping to stay out of Louis' way. In the tenth round Walcott came back strong. There was a numbed silence on the sidewalk under Mr. Kirschner's window. Without saying so, most of the crowd, which had swelled to about twenty, including people not even from our block, began to sense that the title was slipping away from the champion. Walcott came out for the eleventh round full of confidence. He began toying with Louis and went into his famous catwalk, much like Muhammad Ali's shuffle. Louis remained dead serious. He kept stalking Walcott waiting for him to make a mistake. Then it happened. Lightening struck. Boom! Before Wolcott knew what was happening Louis nailed him with a thunderous punch to the chin and quickly followed up with a series of crunching blows to the head. Wolcott went down. He toppled forward, then rolled over on his back. A loud cheer spontaneously erupted from our sidewalk gallery. Then we quickly fell silent again as we listened to referee Frankie Fullam begin the countdown. At the count of SEVEN Walcott was struggling to get up. By the count of EIGHT, NINE he remained helplessly dazed. At the count of TEN Walcott was on all fours attempting to stagger to his feet when he was counted out. With one lightning blow and a few follow-up punches, Louis had come back to defeat "Jersey Joe" Wolcott and retain his title. At thirty-three years of age, a tired but happy Joe Louis announced to the radio audience, "Tonight was my last fight." He went on to say, "I've been around a long time and I think it's about time I quit. And I'm glad to quit with the title still mine."

When the fight was over, at around eleven o'clock, we all slapped each other on the backs. After our initial shouting and joyous celebration died down, some of the older neighbors returned to their apartments. A few of us kids sat down on the curb and, under a starry sky, rehashed each significant moment of the fight until we grew weary from all the excitement and figured it was time to go upstairs to sleep.

As a footnote to Louis's legendary career, it's sad to note that in his later years, after several failed marriages and serious financial difficulties, Louis suffered many mental and physical disorders, possibly related to drug addiction. In his remaining years he was confined to a wheelchair. He died of a heart attack on April 12, 1981 at the age of sixty-six.

It was a wonderful summer night in the Bronx, especially for a kid of fifteen not burdened by thoughts of the future; a kid with no aspirations to become a doctor, lawyer, writer or anything else that required studious application. At this point in my life, no one (including my father, my sister or my relatives in Brooklyn) who observed my aimlessness, would have thought that I would amount to much—including me, if I ever thought about it at all. I was intellectually incurious and baffled by academic subjects, but as much as possible, on the streets, I was having the time of my life. Later on my life turned in a different direction which would have been difficult for anyone to predict.

However, before I grew up, and changed the course of my life, this is how I remember the Bronx and the world I lived in during the 1940s:

The Bronx was sprinkled with candy stores in almost every neighborhood, where a kid could get a black and white ice cream soda, milk shake or malted (with real malt) or, best of all, a six-cent egg cream. It was a place where kids hung out, glancing at comic books looking for the latest issues, and young boys blew straw wrappers into the air and into the faces of their friends. I remember afternoons under a sweltering summer sun, sitting on the curb with my friends, sipping a dripping wet, ice-cold Pepsi or Coke obtained by submerging your hand into a bright red Coca-Cola ice chest positioned outside the front door of the candy store. There were ice cream cones with chocolate sprinkles, Mello-Rolls and Dixie Cups, with lids containing removable transparent waxed- paper printed with photographs of movie stars like Jane Withers, Alice Faye, Dorothy Lamour, and a host of other bright (and not so bright) stars of the Hollywood firmament. And if a small child accidentally dropped the ice cream out of his cone, and he was really polite, the candy store owner would usually replace it free of charge. Games of stickball, punchball, box ball, or stoop ball, played with a "Spaldeen," were ubiquitous during the long, glittering, hot summer days from morning until twilight, when kids reluctantly drifted off the streets, one after the other, to return home for dinner.

An intrinsic part of any game we played in the street was seeing how close you could stand to any passing car that interrupted our game. This was a sport unto itself. In these days we'd make a game out of anything that didn't cost money. The unwritten rule of this game stated that you stand as close as possible to an on-coming automobile—like a matador allowing an on-rushing bull to pass closely in front of him. On our street the bull was two tons of steel and polished chrome moving at fifteen miles per hour. The challenge was to stand as close as possible to the car without letting the fenders hit your knees or allowing one of its tires to roll over your toes. The single most important part of this game of derring-do, was to maintain a disdainful facial expression directed toward the driver of the car who was interrupting our game. For such heroic conduct on the streets of the Bronx you weren't awarded a team letter to sew onto a sweater or a two-tone team jacket with leather elbow patches as was done in college. What you earned, instead, was the unspoken respect and admiration of your friends.

Neighborhoods were patrolled by policemen whom many kids, parents and shop owners thought of as a close relative, maybe someone like their Uncle Dave or Cousin Ralph, all of them looming large in the eyes of young children as the undisputed guardians of law and order. If a child was crying and lost on the hot, sandy beach at Orchard Beach, another child's mother, seeing his plight, would invariably come to his rescue. She would take his hand in hers and help him find his parents or bring him to the Lost and Found section.

New York was a safe place in these days. It was a world festooned with radio heroes and movie stars, and comic book superheroes whose mission in life was to catch criminals, mostly two-bit petty crooks who believed honest people were suckers. Families sat in their living rooms on Sunday mornings reading the funny papers published by the *New York Daily News*. Hollywood fan magazines presented movie stars as ordinary people at home with the same ordinary household chores faced by ordinary American families. Telephone booths with accordion doors for privacy were found on almost every street corner, because many families couldn't afford to have a phone in their home. These were the same telephone booths that guys used to line up dates for Saturday night. And during World War II and immediately after, there was Kate Smith, who could be seen and heard almost everywhere singing *God Bless America,* the country's unofficial national anthem. This was my Bronx. My world. My Shangri-La.

Chapter Twenty-One

One particular Sunday in late August, either 1947 or 1948, my sister, who was now sixteen or seventeen, asked my father if we could go shopping instead of going to a movie. School was starting in a few weeks and she needed some new fall clothes. My father asked her how much money she thought it would take to outfit her. I don't remember the exact amount she told him, but however much it was, my father managed to scrape up the money. My father suggested we meet someplace on the Lower East Side where the stores were open on Sundays because most of them, at that time, were owned by Jews, most of whom closed their shops on Saturday in observance of the Sabbath. And so we met.

After several hours of shopping my father suggested we stop and get something to eat. After that, he said to my sister, if you still need more clothes we'll continue. When my sister walked out of the last store, where she had found many items she liked, including a bright red Chesterfield coat with a black velvet collar, she began to cry.

My father asked her, "Why are you crying?"

"Because you bought me so many clothes."

My father replied, "But that's what you said you needed."

"I know," my sister said," but I really didn't expect you would get me all this."

After my sister stopped crying we walked over to Katz's delicatessen on Houston Street for hot pastrami sandwiches and Dr. Brown's cream soda. I truly believe the visit to Katz's deli was mostly for my benefit as a reward for being so patient while my sister did her back-to-school shopping.

My father's kindness to my sister also extended, from time to time, to some of my friends and even strangers. I can recall a time when he sold—practically gave away—recapped tires to one of my friends, Chuck Del Carpine, and another time to Mr. Costello, the janitor at my high school. My father also managed to buy a car for my best friend Michael—which he "legally" sold to him for one dollar—so he would be able to drive to Maspeth, Queens to visit his high school girlfriend. The car was a fifteen-year-old 1940 powder blue Pontiac which, as it turned out, used more brake fluid than gas, and from time-to-time would lock in third gear. Be that as it may, Michael, an excellent mechanic, managed to keep the car running for over a year until it died a valiant death. Years later, in 1965, I had an opportunity to repeat my father's act of generosity when I sold my Oldsmobile for one dollar to an Italian-born friend of mine, Raffaele Puoti. At the time "Lello" was married (and still is to the same wonderful woman) with a wife and two children to support. After he totaled his brand-new Volkswagen Bug, which he operated without insurance that he couldn't afford, it was difficult, and not safe, for him to get home late at night from his job as a waiter at an up-scale, East Side Italian restaurant in Manhattan.

On another occasion, when my father returned home later than usual, and I asked him why, he told me he picked up a soaking wet colored kid waiting at a bus stop in the rain and drove him home. You could do things like that in these days without fear of being accused as a child molester.

Had my father known of the Roman Emperor, Marcus Aurelius (A.D. 121-180), and read his *Meditations* (as I did at San Francisco State where I did two years of post-graduate work in philosophy), he would have taken great comfort in his writings, for in his own small way my father adhered to many of the teachings professed by the Stoic philosophy, especially when it came to performing random acts of kindness.

> Once you have a done a man a service, what more would you have? Is it not enough to have obeyed the laws of your own nature, without expecting to be paid for it? That is like the eye demanding a reward for seeing, or the feet for walking. It is for that very purpose that they exist; and they have their due in doing what they were created to do. Similarly, man is born for deeds of kindness; and when he has done a kindly action . . . he has done what he was made for, and has received his quittance.

During the 1930s through the 1950s, a parent of one child seemed to be the parent of all children. As I experienced the world at this time, a mother was a mother was a mother. If she saw a child who was not her own, sitting on a curb crying, or who had fallen and scraped his knee or elbow, she would comfort him. An ancient Jewish proverb says: "God could not be everywhere, so he made mothers." One such encounter happened to me when I was living in Sea Gate. It was a warm summer evening and it had already turned dark. Although I was in no particular hurry to get home I decided to run as fast as I could. At some point I slowed down because I didn't want to crash into a middle-aged woman walking toward me on the narrow sidewalk. When I got close to her she took hold of my arm and said in a very caring voice, "You're perspiring. Are you running because something frightened you?" How could I possibly explain to her I was eight years old and was running for the sheer joy of it? I told her I was fine and continued running until I reached home.

Mothers during these times seemed to show the same concern and compassion for all children regardless, pretty much, of race or ethnicity. A child was a child was a child. As a kid it was comforting to know you could go up to just about any adult or police officer and say, "I'm lost," or "I need a nickel to take the trolley home" . . . as I once had to do after traveling by myself into Manhattan to see *The Pride of the Yankees* when I was nine or ten years old. I was spending the summer at Aunt Lee's at the time and no one would take me to see this movie about baseball legend Lou Gehrig. I was determined to see it, so I decided to go by myself. I may not even have told anyone I was going. I also don't remember how I got into the theater that day without being accompanied by an adult, but knowing me I probably asked someone on line to buy my ticket.

If you want to get a sense of this relatively gentle bygone era, watch the movie *The Little Fugitive* (d: Ashley, Engel & Orkin,1953), a documentary-style film made on a shoestring budget by a husband and wife team of professional photographers. It tells the story of a seven-year-old kid who runs away from home for the better part of two days after he is tricked into thinking he has killed his older brother. He ends up in Coney Island, where his fear and guilt is soon forgotten as he enjoys one amusement after the other, and stuffs his face with hot dogs, pop corn, cotton candy and soda pop before his money runs out. You get the sense that although he is on his own, he's really not, because the adult world he encounters -- inhabited by mothers, policemen, park employees—is not at all threatening. And when his older brother, the perpetrator of this prank, discovers he's run away to Coney Island he goes in search of him. It was a wonderful time to grow up in New York and this little movie captures the innocence that marked that era. The year the film was released it won the Venice Film Festival's Silver Lion award.

Chapter Twenty-Two

In 1947, when I was fourteen and in the eighth grade at P. S. 16, my father was sixty-one, which was considered old in those days. He mentioned to me that he wasn't feeling well which was a rare admittance for him. I had never heard him complain about anything, let alone his health—and neither one of us had visited a doctor's office since we had moved to the Bronx. However, I was aware that there was a cottage on a small lot across the street from our apartment house with a signpost announcing a doctor's office. In those days you didn't need to make an appointment; you just dropped in and waited your turn. The next day my father came home earlier than usual and together we walked over to the office. After the doctor had asked him a few questions and examined him I asked:

"What's wrong with my father?"

"He has arteriosclerosis.

"What's that?"

"It's a hardening or narrowing of the arterial walls that feed blood to the heart."

"What causes that?"

"The walls can get clogged by the foods we eat that build up plaque, like the plaque that builds up on your teeth that you to try to brush away. Or sometimes the body itself produces plaque."

"So what kind of medicine can you give him?"

A grave visage settled over his face before he replied: "I'm afraid we don't have any medicine for his condition."

Even though I was asking the questions while my father was getting dressed, we both heard the doctor's response to my last question—and I think we both knew he had just been handed a death sentence. My father paid the doctor and thanked him, and then we left the office, walked across the street, and mounted the stairs to our apartment. Neither one of us knew what to say, so we didn't speak about it. But I knew from the look on my father's face, that he knew he was living on borrowed time from here on out. I, on the other hand, thought only of myself. What if he dropped dead tomorrow, or next week or next month? What would happen to me? Where would I go? Who would look after me? The darkest fear that crossed my mind was that I would be sent to a state-run orphanage until I was eighteen, and that scared the crap out of me. As it turned out, my father did die of a heart attack, but not until eleven years later. During all that time I never heard him complain, and he made no concessions to his condition. I think he naturally followed the code he had lived by all his life. As long as there was breath in him, he continued to meet adversity head on, and nothing prevented him from looking after me and my sister. He didn't know any other way to live. On the morning that he died of a massive heart attack he was on the way out of the house to go to work.

After the doctor's grim diagnosis, I lived for the next six months with the fear that my father might die any moment. On one occasion, when I was walking home from P.S. 16 at three o'clock in the afternoon, I heard the wailing sound of a siren coming from an ambulance and I panicked, imagining that it was racing through traffic to reach my apartment house, to rescue my father. I was half way home, on Richardson Avenue, when I heard the siren. I immediately began to run toward our apartment house convinced that my father had had a heart attack and someone had called the police or the hospital. As I was running, I envisioned my father strapped to a stretcher and being carried down the front steps of our apartment house with all the kids and neighbors looking on. As I breathlessly turned the corner where we lived I was overcome with relief when I saw there was no ambulance in front of my house, just a bunch of kids playing ball in the street and mothers heading upstairs, their arms loaded down with brown grocery bags.

In 1996 I was diagnosed with the same heart condition that my father had had. I had high cholesterol and was prescribed Lipitor, which, along with diet and exercise, has kept my cholesterol level pretty much in check. In 2002, however, I had an angioplasty to correct a severely occluded artery. This procedure, along with Lipitor, was not available in 1947. Over the years I've had a few scary moments, but each time it turned out that my discomfort was caused, not by my heart but by a temporary stomach disorder that can produce difficult-to-diagnose aches and pains, particularly in the chest and intestines. Among Jews this condition is often referred to as a "nervous stomach."

To this day, if my wife or one of my daughters gets sick, I worry that they will die just like my mother did. My anxiety about my daughters' health and safety grew more pronounced after my divorce when, for the next twenty years, I was living by myself, and the girls were on their own. One of the ways that my anxiety shows up, then and now, is the way I check my phone messages as soon as I get home, even if I am gone only a short while. When there are no messages, I breath a deep sigh of relief. I can't bear to think that some tragedy may have befallen them and that I wasn't available, *at that exact moment,* to be there for them. (Cell phones weren't on the market in those earlier days.) It's clear to me that my mother's early death compounded any normal parental anxiety.

Also, for many years, if the telephone rang at home after nine o'clock in the evening, I would imagine the worst before I picked up the receiver. To this day, there are times I wake up in the middle of the night because I think I heard the phone ring. Thanks to Jean and her understanding—and her gallows humor, which matches mine—my behavior is less neurotic than it used to be. I still reach for the phone when I come home, but it's no longer with the same degree of urgency.

As I write these words, I realize just how strongly my mother's death has affected me. The trauma of her actual death—and the repeated nightmarish dreams of watching her drown in a sea of mud and my not being able to save her—has left me with more emotional scars than I care to think about. Add to this my adolescent years of worrying about my father's impending death from heart disease, and it's not surprising that, as far back as I can remember, I have always been waiting and worrying for the other shoe to drop.

To help bring a little levity to my tendency to worry too much, I like to tell the following story:

Two Jewish mobsters in Chicago were given a contract to murder Al Capone. To figure out the best way to carry out their assignment, they scrupulously observed his every move for two weeks. They discovered that he followed a fairly rigid routine. They decided the best place to kill him was when he returned to his apartment, which he did every night at 6 p.m. on the dot. On the appointed day they arrived at his apartment house fifteen minutes early to make sure they had plenty of time to get in position. The hallway outside his apartment door was dimly lit so they hid in the shadows waiting for him to arrive, checking their weapons several times to make sure nothing would go wrong.

Mobster #1
What time is it?

Mobster #2
Six o'clock.

Mobster #1
He should be here any minute.

Mobster # 2
Don't worry. He'll be here.

Mobster #1
What time is it?

Mobster # 2
Six fifteen.

Mobster #1
He should have been here by now.

Mobster # 2
Be patient. He'll show up.

Mobster #1
What time is it?

Mobster #2
Six thirty.

Mobster # 1
Gee, I hope nothing happened to him.

Chapter Twenty-Three

In 1950,when I was approaching seventeen, my father, who was under near constant pleading for him to buy me a car which he could ill afford, managed to find one on the lot of one of his used car customers. It was a 1938 Oldsmobile. Naturally, I was thrilled to have my own car even if it was twelve years' old. But I was disappointed about one thing—which I never shared with my father—and that was that it didn't have a radio. Without a radio, my adolescent mind lamented, how was I ever going to get my dates "in the mood?" I thought I needed help from Tony Bennett singing *Because of You*, or the smooth styling of Billy Eckstine singing *My Foolish Heart* or *I Apologize*, or Sarah Vaughn singing *Tenderly*, Buddy Clark crooning *You're Breaking My Heart*, or the "Singin' Rage" Miss Patti Page doing her sentimental version of *So in Love*. As it turned out, I managed to capture a few kisses without the radio.

One summer night, shortly after I got the car and earned my junior driver's license (which stipulated that kids between the ages of sixteen and eighteen were not allowed to drive at night) I took off after dinner with three of the guys from my block, all of them members of my Pontiac baseball team. (Thinking of my team brings back a memory of when I was fifteen and my father bought me my first pair of baseball shoes, or "cleats," as we called them. After dinner one night he took me to Davega's sporting goods store on Fordham Road and allowed me to pick out the pair I wanted. This was a big deal to me. It was a step up from playing baseball in sneakers. To my mind, if you owned a pair of "cleats" you were no longer a kid.)

Now, getting back to my nocturnal escapade with my friends. Ritchie Schultz sat in the front. He played center field and was the best player on our team. Roddy Rowan, the best shortstop on any team in our area, sat in the back with Vito Schlangapori, our slugging left fielder. Walter Gaga, the team's catcher, was not with us that evening. Catching was the only position he could play because he had a clubfoot. Walter had a powerful upper body and a strong right arm so he was good at throwing guys out who attempted to steal second base. He was a good hitter too. It just took him forever to hop and skip to reach first base.

We headed out to Playland in Rye Beach in Westchester County with the perennial hope of meeting some girls. On the way back home at about 10 p.m., after a luckless evening, I was driving up Huguenot Street in New Rochelle. There was a huge Rheingold beer truck in front of me moving very slowly up a long, low-lying hill. Foolishly, I edged my car out toward the double yellow lines to peek around the truck. When I saw there was no oncoming traffic I threw the car into second gear and illegally crossed over the double yellow lines (on a curve, no less) speeding around the lumbering beer truck. No sooner had I accomplished this impressive maneuver than I heard a police siren and became aware of red flashing lights in my rear view mirror, so I pulled over to the side of the curb awaiting the inevitable. Sure enough, I got a ticket. Then the policeman said I would have to leave the car there since I was not allowed to drive at night with a junior license. Not wanting to leave my car in New Rochelle, and having no way to get back to the Bronx, I explained to the police officer that Ritchie was eighteen and asked if he could drive the car. The officer reluctantly agreed, and we were once again on our way.

During the ride back to the Bronx there was quite a bit of discussion in the car about how I was going to tell my father I had gotten a ticket. I wasn't sure what his response might be to my "brush with the law," but one thing I knew for sure, he would want me to tell him the truth. When we finally arrived back home my friends left and I locked the car doors and went upstairs. When I entered our apartment the light was still on in the kitchen. There was my father seated at the table reading his newspaper, the World-Telegram & Sun, and finishing off a bottle of Tudor beer. As on so many other occasions when I had been out late, my father stayed up until I arrived home safely. I tried to be as nonchalant as possible when I sat down across from him. He asked me if I had had a good time. I said yes, and then said, "I have something to tell you."

"What is it," he asked.

"I got a ticket on the way home tonight."

"Well," he said, "you were bound to get your first ticket sooner or later."

That was it. That's all he said. No yelling. No lecturing. I distinctly remember feeling an immense sense of relief; but more than that, I remember thinking to myself that when I got older and had kids of my own, this was exactly how I was going to handle things. I remember that I didn't thank my father for being so understanding. I felt that any expression of gratitude would be missing the point. He was trying to teach me a lesson and gratitude had nothing to do with it. If I had thanked him for not being angry he probably would have said, "What's to get upset about. A ticket is not the end of the world. As long as you didn't get hurt. Just be more careful next time." Or he might have said what he had told me once before: "In this world you have to be a boy first before you can be a man."

Another time, when I was about sixteen, I was out with some new friends, guys in their twenties, at a polka party at a Polish center in Yonkers. They didn't drop me off at my house until 2 a.m. When we approached my apartment house I saw my father standing on the corner waiting for me. I will never forget the grim expression on his face—a look of unbearable worry and fear. (Had we been able to afford a phone I would have called him.) When I got out of the car I felt terrible that I had caused him such grievous pain. I think he was so relieved to see me he didn't say a word. Taking care of me was his life. He couldn't afford to lose me. After I had apologized we trudged upstairs, one behind the other, and wordlessly got undressed and into bed. The next morning he never said a word about it. But his presence on the street corner at 2 a.m. taught me a lesson about love and caring and consideration for others that I have never forgotten.

Over the years I gradually grew accustomed to the idea that I could tell my father anything without being afraid that he would lose his temper. During my growing-up years I recall that my love for my father went beyond that of the usual filial relationship. My father was much more to me than just my father. In his own quiet way he was also a teacher whom I admired and respected—even though there had been times when I was younger that I had felt embarrassed because he was so much older than my friends' parents.

In the late 1940s my father, still looking to strike it rich, continued perfecting one or more of his inventions. One summer night I came home at about nine or ten o'clock and found my father seated at the kitchen table with his wire cutters, files, shears and a small vice secured to the table. As soon as I walked into the kitchen I could tell he was giddy with excitement over the progress he had made that evening on one of his inventions (I think it was the metal clamp that facilitated pumping air into rubber tire tubes), and he couldn't wait to share the news with me. He was so full of joy at the prospect of certain success, that he actually sang and danced around the kitchen in a manner not unlike the unforgettable jig Walter Huston performed in *The Treasure of the Sierra Madre* (d: John Huston, 1948) when he and his fellow prospectors discovered gold in the Sierra mountains.

Chapter Twenty-Four

Shortly after we moved to the Bronx, I became friendly with a kid my age who lived across the court in building 708. His name was Jerry Gilberg. He played first base for our Pontiac baseball team. His parents had the distinction of being the first family in our apartment house to own a television set. In 1948 they bought a Dumont TV with a five-inch screen. To increase the size of the picture, Jerry's father (who drove a truck delivering laundry to retail businesses) purchased a piece of convex plastic that snapped on to the front of the screen. But this only enlarged the picture if you sat directly in front of the TV. If you sat off to either side the picture was badly distorted. On Tuesday nights Jerry's parents would invite six or seven people from the building to come over to watch Milton Berle, "Mr. Television," on the Texaco Star Theater at eight o'clock. Mrs. Gilberg always asked me to bring my father along, but he routinely declined telling me to go ahead over and have a good time. He preferred to enjoy his solitude in our apartment reading his newspaper and sipping a glass of beer.

Jerry's mother would set up folding chairs in the living room for her guests. Before the show began she'd turn off the lights. She felt sitting in a darkened room helped create the same magical atmosphere experienced in movie theaters. When the show was over everyone stood up and thanked Jerry's parents and returned to their own apartments having enjoyed the vaudeville-style antics of "Uncle Miltie." You could tell they also left with a sense of wonder at the miracle of modern science. One of the guests would invariably say about the magic of television, "What will they think of next?"

When I was about fourteen, Jerry introduced me to a bunch of Jewish kids living in Mt. Vernon. I spent considerable time with them in the wholesome atmosphere of the Young Men's Hebrew Association (YMHA) on Tenth Street—about a ten or fifteen-minute trolley car ride from my apartment house. Unlike those few of us who lived in the Bronx, the guys from Mt. Vernon all lived in comfortable single-family homes with landscaped front lawns, roomy backyards, formal dining rooms, living rooms with a fireplace, separate bedrooms, and knotty pine breakfast nooks in the kitchen. And there was a mother in every one of these homes. Like the Jewish kids I knew in Sea Gate, many of them came from middle or upper-middle-class families. Almost all of them were good students and were raised with the expectation that they would attend college. The splendid sounding colleges they considered had names like Colgate, Bucknell, Oberlin, Tufts, Brown and Lehigh. The only colleges I had ever heard about were ones that you travelled to by subway and had plebeian names like City College, Queens College, Brooklyn College, Manhattan College or Hunter College. You also traveled to Columbia by subway, and even I knew this was some place special and you had to be incredibly smart to get in there.

None of my Mt. Vernon friends flaunted the fact that their families were well-off enough to purchase nice clothes, buy new cars and take family vacations during the summer. What bothered me most—what I envied most—was their sense of entitlement, the casual attitude and self-assuredness with which they accepted their fortunate circumstances without giving any thought (as far as I could tell) as to how the "other half" lived, namely me. While I was growing up, whether it was in Sea Gate or hanging out with these Mt. Vernon kids, I was always aware of a line between the "haves" and the "have-nots," and there was no mistaking the fact that I was on the side of the "have-nots." Consequently, I often felt uncomfortable— like a trespasser—in their presence.

When I would think about "out-of-state" schools my mind would conjure up images of June Allyson and Peter Lawford dancing and singing their way through Tate U. performing such memorable numbers as *Varsity Drag* and *Pass That Peace Pipe* in the MGM musical *Good News* (d: Charles Watters, 1947). I envisioned all out-of-state schools to be just like the one in this movie, with ivy-covered walls, tree-lined walkways, bicycle paths, frat houses, dorms where everyone had his own desk to study at, and of course a huge track and field stadium and a top notch football team. As much as there was a part of me that wanted to attend one of these schools, I knew that the possibility was remote. I felt certain I wasn't smart enough, or, rich enough, and, in a certain sense, not even physically suited for this kind of campus life. I couldn't picture myself going out for their football or basketball teams, or throwing a javelin, discus or shot-put, or using a bamboo pole to hurl my body over a fifteen-foot bar in a pole vault competition. These organized sports were alien to me. I grew up playing street games.

Most often the teenage girls at the Y were only interested in dating college men and high school jocks from Mt. Vernon, sporting suede bucs or brown and white saddle shoes. How many times did I hear from one of these girls, "You're from where? The Bronx? " Then they would politely disappear. However, there was one girl I met who was not at all like this. Her name was Marcia Werbler, a very bright young lady who came, as far as I could tell, from an upper middle class family and didn't belong to any cliques at Mt. Vernon high school. Marcia was slender, with a comely appearance and a refreshing lack of pretension. One of the things I liked best about her was that when she spoke to you, she looked directly at you. Her eyes didn't dart around the room looking at other guys she thought might be more in-teresting. She simply had this way about her that made you feel important; that there was no one else she would rather be talk-ing to at the moment. On the downside, however, Marcia was at least two inches taller than me, which led to a rather awkward and embarrassing situation. At the time I met her I was already in my second year of high school.

I remember how I struggled to find the courage to ask her out on a date. When I eventually did, to my great surprise, she accepted. The date was set for a Saturday. Our plan was to go to Manhattan on the New York Central Railroad, boarding at the Mt. Vernon station, and see a movie and stage show at the Para-mount Theater. I picked her up at her home around eleven a.m. Her house was one of those lovely old-fashioned Westchester

Tudors situated directly across the street from Hartley Park on Lincoln Avenue near Gramatan Circle. The house, with its steep pitched slate roof, was set back from the street amidst mature trees and bushes that were trimmed and pruned with meticulous care, reflecting the attention of a professional gardener. A winding slate path led up to the front door.

I remember the rest of this story as if it had taken place yesterday. When we arrived at the Paramount Theater, Marcia politely stood off to the side of the ticket booth to let me carry out the manly task of purchasing our tickets. Inside the booth sat a middle-aged, overweight, dour-faced woman. I passed my money to her under the glass window and asked for two tickets. The woman asked me how old I was. I told her sixteen. She said I didn't look sixteen, and she wouldn't sell me a ticket unless I was accompanied by an adult. Careful not to draw Marcia's attention to my predicament, I argued my case with this intractable ticket seller. When my arguments proved ineffective, I tried to appeal to her sympathy by telling her I was on a date and how would it look if I had to tell my date—"who's standing right over there"—nodding my head inconspicuously in Marcia's direction, that we couldn't get into the theater because I didn't look old enough. My appeal for an exemption fell on deaf ears.

While this discourse was taking place I was aware that Marcia was only a few feet away, but hopefully out of earshot. I would have been crushed had she heard what was going on between me and this odious ticket agent. At one point I sensed the hopelessness of my situation which set my mind spinning in search of some plausible way to save myself from total humiliation. For a moment, I thought about telling Marcia the next show was sold out, but not to worry, we could walk down the street and try our luck at the Capitol or Roxy. I decided against this however, because suddenly I was exhausted by the entire ordeal. All I wanted to do was find a hole in the sidewalk, crawl into it and disappear. Unfortunately, the city of New York did not provide any underground escape hatches for people in my circumstance. My only hope at this point was that there was some truth to the maxim, "Honesty is the best policy." (After all, it always worked with my father!) Having reconciled myself to my fate, I walked over to Marcia, who was patiently awaiting my return, and told her what had happened. "How ridiculous," she said in a most straightforward manner. Without making me feel worse than I already did, she politely asked me to give her the money for the tickets and she would purchase them—which she did unceremoniously.

Although I was grateful to Marcia for the way she handled this delicate situation, my afternoon was ruined. I mean, how do you dare put your arm around a girl who just got you into the movies after you had been refused admission because you didn't look old enough to be allowed in without an adult. When we came out of the theater we stopped for something to eat and then took the subway over to Grand Central Station to head back home to Mt. Vernon. As hard as she tried to ignore my embarrassment, I couldn't escape my own miserable feelings. I had all I could do to uphold my half of our stilted conversation until we got back to her house. I walked her to the front door and thanked her for a great time, secretly hoping I would never have to see her again, which I never did.

It's strange, though, that after all these years, it is not the embarrassment I suffered that stands out in my memory, but my recollection of Marcia's gracious behavior, which serves to confirm that my initial instincts were right about her being a great girl!

On the basketball court at the Y I was more sure of myself. My mind was on sports and not girls, or cars or school or lack of money. Because I was one of the shorter kids at the Y, I wasn't the best basketball player around, but I held my own. I had a pretty good two-handed set shot, which was the norm at this time, and my percentage at the free-throw line was better than most. I knew it was futile to try to muscle my way under the boards to fight for rebounds against much bigger guys. But what I lacked in height and brute strength I made up for in alertness, in setting plays and spotting the open man driving toward the basket. I was also a strong voice championing team spirit.

Mo Davis was the basketball instructor and athletic director at the Y. He was one of the most decent, fair-minded people I ever met. I remember one day during a basketball game one of the players stuck his leg out to trip another player running past him. Mo was furious—madder than I'd ever seen him before. He blew his whistle loud and long to stop the game right then and there. He instructed all of us— not just the guilty kid—to sit down on the sidelines. He then went into a lecture about fair play and sportsmanship. The thing I liked best about how Mo handled the situation, is that he didn't direct his comments at the guilty player, which would have only embarrassed him further in front of the rest of us. Instead, he looked into the faces of each and every one of us during his strongly worded outpouring. When the lecture was over, he blew his whistle and said, "Okay, now. Let's play ball."

In 1948, when I was fifteen, the YMHA presented me with the Lt. Milton Herman Award. My father and sister were present at a small ceremony held on the evening of March 3 in the Y lounge, at which time I was lauded by several board members and presented with an inscribed trophy. The inscription read: "Stephen is one of the more popular boys around the Y, and has been selected because of his general helpfulness, loyalty, and future leadership ability." The award, which included three weeks free at camp Willoway, the YMHA summer camp, was given yearly in memory of Lt. Milton Herman, who gave his life in the service of his country in World War II.

Camp was fun. I got to play softball, basketball and handball almost every day. I also got to go canoeing, which was an entirely new experience for me. I enjoyed the food, and the counselors were great. But one night, during my last week at camp, some of my bunkmates and I got into a little trouble. A few of the guys in my cabin decided to raid the girls' side of the camp in the middle of the night. This top-secret mission was called a "panty raid," which I later learned was camp lingo for stealing girls' underwear. The plan was for all the guys in our cabin, about fifteen of us, to get up at midnight and sneak around the perimeter of the campgrounds to reach the paved road that separated the boys' camp from the girls'. There was a much shorter route, but it would have meant walking through the middle of the campgrounds, past the cabins where some of the staff members and counselors slept. It was decided that the shortcut was too risky. As midnight approached, one of the leaders of this mission got up from his bunk bed and whispered: "All right, guys. It's time to go." I had never been part of an organized secret mission like this before, so it all seemed very exciting. I felt like a member of some specially trained World War II military unit, where each guy was hand-picked because he possessed a certain skill that was vital to the success of the operation.

The first part of our plan was executed with military precision. We successfully reached the paved road just outside the boys' campground without being spotted. On both sides of the road stood tall trees and thick shrubs, a perfect camouflage, I imagined, for an ambush by enemy soldiers. Scenes from the movie *The Fighting Seabees* (d: Edward Ludwig, 1944) came to mind. I felt as though John Wayne, fearless leader in the movies (and draft dodger in real life), was leading us on a night-time mission through dense jungle to destroy enemy soldiers who were hiding behind bushes and in treetops ready to pick us off in the moonlight like sitting ducks. Unlike the movie, however, we didn't have bulldozers rigged with machine guns to ensure our success. Our best chance for success was the element of *surprise!* Before long we reached the girls' camp, and here's where our scheme fell apart, since no one had bothered to plan what we were supposed to do once we reached the target area. It quickly became apparent that the best strategy was every man for himself. A few of us stuck together and stealthily approached a particular cabin as our target. Our plan was to sneak inside and find a pair of panties, a bra, or the top of a bathing suit, any article of girls' clothing associated with female sexuality—which, at our age, could have been just about anything that touched their skin.

Once our mission was accomplished, we planned to sneak back to base. But since we weren't the professionals we thought we were, our stumbling around in the dark woke up the girls and in seconds our plans turned into pandemonium. The girls jumped out of their bunks and started yelling, "RAID! RAID!" At this point the element of surprise had been lost. The enemy had spotted us and opened fire with their flashlights. "Let's get out of here," one of my fellow conspirators yelled. Like wild horses we hightailed it across the paved road and took the short cut back to our cabin without bothering to calculate the risk of being spotted. We ran through the darkened campgrounds whizzing past trees and cabins where campers and counselors were fast asleep. I was in the middle of the pack as we raced onward. As we passed the camp director's cabin, I saw, out of the corner of my eye, that the director had joined our pack—chasing us from behind in his bathrobe and slippers with flashlight in hand. I kept on running as fast as I could knowing full well we had been caught red-handed, even if none of the other guys had yet realized this fact.

As soon as we reached our cabin someone yelled, "Quick. Get under the covers and make believe you're asleep." Knowing what I already knew, I realized this ploy had the same chance of success as our original plan. But having no other options, I followed the directive from this anonymous voice along with everyone else. Within a few seconds the camp director, huffing and puffing, stumbled into our cabin and said: "Okay, everybody up and out of bed. Let's go. You're not fooling anyone, boys, especially me. Into the dining room, all of you." And then to my astonishment he turned to me and said, "Until I find out differently, I'm assuming you were the one who organized this activity. You're too bright to be a follower." I don't know what gave him this impression, unless he assumed one of two things: either he thought I was brighter than the other boys because I had received the Lt. Milton Herman Award—in which case I would have reminded him that my award was for *future* leadership ability, not *immediate* leadership ability at the age of fifteen—or, he may have figured that, because I was from the Bronx (you know, where *devious activities* take place all the time), it was likely that I would be the one to organize some sort of mischief. In the dining room that night we got a good talking to by the camp director. The next morning our escapade was the talk of the camp. By afternoon, however, camp life was pretty much back to normal. No one had been blindfolded and lined up against a wall and shot and no letters were sent home to parents to inform them of their kids' disreputable behavior. For me, it was an exciting, harmless adventure that I chalked up as part of a great summer experience.

This was the first and only time I ever attended sleep-away camp. As much as I enjoyed myself those three weeks, I felt that deep down I really didn't belong there, with kids whose families could afford to send them away for four or six weeks every summer. On visitors' weekend, their parents drove up in new cars to spend the day with their kids and to socialize with the other parents, most of whom they already knew from high school meetings, business associations and from the synagogues or temples where they congregated to celebrate the High Holy Days. My father also showed up, but he, not knowing any of the other parents, pretty much stayed to himself watching us play a soft ball game. After the game I sat down with him for lunch in the general mess hall.

For my friends and their parents, the Y summer camp was an extension of their socially integrated lives, but it was not my life, even though there were times I wished it were. After my camp days were over I returned to the Bronx where I felt at home, where I belonged. Over the next week or so I went through a period of introspection. The question I put to myself was this: Should I remain loyal to my Jewish friends in Mt. Vernon or should I join up with some guys from the Bronx— all of them Italian from blue-collar families. It was my best friend from grammar school and high school, Michael Mosia, who introduced me to them. The group included Lou Zaccaro, Don Di Lorenzo, Neal Maffeo, Don Cruciani, Mike Calabro, Ralph Vellone, Cosmo Del Carpine, Ray Consilvio, Nick Marsh, Joe "Archie" Arcieri, and Johnny Reda, a guy my size who was soft-spoken and easy-going until he got mad, at which point he could take on five or ten guys at the same time and beat the crap out of half of them.

I decided to go Italian. Like me, most of them lived in apartment houses, or rented the upstairs or downstairs of a two-family home near White Plains Road between 216th and 219th Streets. These were guys from working-class families who would give you the shirt off their backs (which I didn't need, but at one point I did need a pair of their shiny black shoes, the kind they wore to church every Sunday dressed in their navy blue suits). I immediately fell in with these guys, and I was grateful to them for accepting and befriending me. Many years later they formally acknowledged my status as "one of them." This was accomplished by incorporating the star of David into the middle of a Christian cross appearing on a crest designed by Mike Calabro. The official crest was stitched in the upper right-hand corner of our silver and blue jackets, identifying us as members of our very own social club, the "Jammas."

About the black shoes: Ralph loaned me his pair to wear the night of my high school prom because I owned only two pair of shoes, one brown and the other cordovan, neither of which would work with the tuxedo I had rented. As it turned out, the shoes he loaned me were too large so I had to stuff newspapers in the toe to keep them from slipping off my feet. An image of Charlie Chaplin crossed my mind. All of this was done at the last minute since Michael and I only decided to attend our prom at two o'clock that afternoon. The prom was held at the Hotel Pierre on Central Park West. Neither one of us could round up dates that late in the day. I ended up taking Michael's older sister, Marie (who was dead tired after working all day at her secretarial job in Manhattan), and he took her girlfriend, Marie Cereito. Michael spent most of the evening dancing with his future wife, Norma, and told her date, Sal Pertara, to behave himself when he took her home.

As Humphrey Bogart said to Claude Rains in the closing scene of *Casablanca*, "Louie, I think this is the beginning of a beautiful friendship." It was, and still is. To this day, for the past twenty-five years, we all get together for an annual July 4th barbecue party and reunion at Ralph's home in Rye, New York.

▲ Me at sixteen.

▲ Mike and I at seventeen.

▲ Me in the Navy, circa 1952.

Mike and I in mid-life, circa 1996.

Some of my Bronx buddies in mid-life. Standing from left to right: Ralph Vellone, Mike Calabro, Mike Mosia. Seated from left to right: Tony Praino, Donald Di Lorenzo, Lou Zaccaro, me, circa 1985.

Me with my arms around
Aunt Lee and Cousin
Ruth. Daughter Julie in the
foreground, circa 1966.

Getting ready to go joggin with my daughters Julie,
left, and Tracy, circa 1971.

Me with my daughters all grown up, circa 1985.

My sister and I, circa 1990.

▲ Jean and I on our wedding day, November 26, 2004.

▲ Jean and I in 2014.

Chapter Twenty-Five

In 1947, Michael and I graduated from P.S. 16. We both decided, for slightly different reasons, that we didn't want to attend De Witt Clinton, an all-boys high school. I didn't want to go there because I felt academically unprepared for courses in science, advanced mathematics and possibly a foreign language. Instead, Michael and I applied for acceptance to the School of Industrial Arts (SIA) in Manhattan. To be accepted you had to take an entrance exam, part of which was to draw a picture of a man on a street corner selling fruits and vegetables from a pushcart. It would appear that my practice of drawing comic book characters when I was younger finally paid off. Math was another part of the exam, a subject I was not very good at, so Michael allowed me to look over his shoulder to copy the correct answers. Several weeks later, despite his help, I learned I had not been accepted, but he had been. When I was informed of the school's decision, I was crestfallen, so much so that one of my teachers intervened on my behalf. As luck would have it, one of the women administrators at my school was the sister of Anita B. Kronk, the assistant to the principal of SIA. I assume she placed a call to her sister to request an exception in my case, and I was soon told that the school had reversed its decision and granted my acceptance. I was one happy kid!

SIA's annex building originally served as a civil war hospital. Over the years it had been modified many times. You could still get a feel for its historic past as you moved through its architectural twists and turns and narrow passageways, and the outdoor steel catwalks we walked on to get to our classrooms. We were schooled for two years at the annex during which time we were offered courses in a variety of artistic fields, including drafting, illustration, fashion design, window decoration, cartooning, sculpture and photography. At the end of two years we were required to choose a major. By the time I had to make this decision, I was convinced that I lacked the talent to become a commercial artist. I simply had to observe my gifted classmates to come to this realization. Many of these kids could do more with two colored pencils than I could possibly do with a dozen colored pencils, Speedball pens, pastels and tempera paints. Although I couldn't draw as well as many of my classmates, I discovered that I had a keen eye for design, an ability I cultivated and made use of later in life in the advertising field (and when I redesigned my new home after the original house burned to the ground in the massive Oakland Hills fire of 1991).

One of the things I liked most about SIA was that it was a cultural melting pot. It drew students from every one of the five boroughs in New York and included Negroes (before the term "blacks" or "African Americans" became accepted terms),

Puerto Ricans, Italians, Jews and Irish, mostly from working class families. Most amazing of all is the fact that I don't recall any instances of racial or ethnic tension at our school. Perhaps it was our love of art, and our daily involvement in a creative process, that transcended any differences that might otherwise have surfaced. Being located in Manhattan made it possible and convenient for the school to arrange field trips to many of the city's museums—Guggenheim, Whitney, Metropolitan Museum of Art, Museum of Modern Art—which was an education in and of itself. Another one of my best friends from SIA, Tomaso "Tom" Puliafito, became a professor of art at Pratt Institute (where he did his undergraduate work) and in his prime in the late nineteen seventies had several of his pieces on exhibit in the Whitney. Jean and I visit Tom and his wife, Pat, on our annual 4th of July reunion in New York, and he's still turning out fantastic pieces of contemporary art.

The annex was located on 51st Street between Lexington and Park Avenue—a few blocks from St. Patrick's Cathedral. To get to the annex I would take the express train from the Bronx to 42nd Street, then take a local train one stop back to 51st Street. To get to the main building on 79th Street between Third and Second Avenues, I would take the same White Plains Road train to the Gun Hill or Fordham Road station where I would change over to the Third Avenue El. The black cars on the El were much older than the subway cars. At each end of one of these cars there was an electric fan hanging from the ceiling, with two more additional fans located near the middle section. A series of leather straps hung down from a horizontal bar that extended the length of the car allowing standing passengers to brace themselves as the train rounded corners and stopped and started with a jerk. Behind and above the hand straps, along the sides of the car, there was a row of bare light bulbs with an additional row of light bulbs running down the center of the arched ceiling. Between each car was a small open platform enclosed by a wrought iron gate. This was my favorite place to stand in the spring and early fall months, because from here I could look down at the people and shops below—from thirty feet above ground—as the train rattled along Third Avenue. The train stations along the line recalled an earlier era going back before the turn of the century. The waiting rooms featured dark wood-paneled walls, potbellied stoves, heavy wooden turnstiles and a clerk who sat inside a change booth behind a glass window dispensing coins to passengers. He would slide the coins into a shallow shell-shaped wooden receptacle worn smooth over the years from fingers rubbing the wooden surface to collect the correct change. On cold, blustery days if, for one reason or another, I found myself shivering inside one of these antiquated waiting rooms, I enjoyed conjuring up the feeling of what it would have been like to live in that earlier time.

I learned many things about art at SIA. I also learned about the art of kissing. I was taught by Angie Soresse who gave me private lessons after school, (and occasionally on stairwells during school lunch hour.) Angie was an olive-skinned Italian girl who lived in Manhattan on 112th Street near Second Avenue in a section called Spanish Harlem, previously an all-Italian neighborhood. Angie was about five foot three, exquisitely proportioned with black hair, high cheekbones and the most alluring eyes of any girl I had ever known.

One day when I was about sixteen, Angie and I decided to cut our afternoon classes and go to a movie at the Trans-Lux movie theater just down the street from the main building. I have absolutely no recollection of the movie we went to see, probably because I don't remember ever looking up at the screen after watching the first few minutes. Angie and I sat in the last row of the balcony, and before long I planted my best kiss on her with my lips, as usual, tightly sealed. Seconds later, under Angie's gentle prodding, my lips parted and I felt her tongue inside my mouth, a sensation that made me dizzy with desire. I don't remember how long we remained in the theater on this wintery afternoon, but it was getting late by the time we decided to leave. As we exited the theater Angie said goodbye and headed for the subway. "If I don't get home before dark my mother will kill me," she said as we parted. I couldn't imagine what her mother would have done to her if she had known she had cut class and spent the afternoon making out with some guy at the movies.

After she walked away I stood there on the sidewalk trying to figure out what had just transpired in that darkened movie theater. No clarifying thoughts came to mind, but I remember how my legs were trembling as I started walking toward the Third Avenue El station to head for the Bronx. I remember the train was crowded with adults returning home from work and all the seats were taken. I was hoping someone would get up so I could sit down, because I wasn't sure my rubbery legs would support me all the way home.

On the ride home I remember my thoughts turned to Barbara Roth, an SIA classmate from Queens whom I had dated frequently before I had met Angie. I liked Barbara a lot, and we had gone to the movies quite a few times on Saturday nights. After the movies we would head back to her house and if her parents weren't home we would sit on the living room couch and "make out." What I remember most about these encounters was the way I kissed her with my lips tightly sealed. No matter how hard I pressed my lips against hers I always felt like I was kissing a lamppost. I knew something was missing, but I couldn't figure out what it was. It wasn't until my cinematic experience with Angie that I realized what I was doing wrong—and why Barbara had dumped me for an older guy of nineteen who obviously knew what kissing was all about.

Chapter Twenty-Six

On unbearably hot, humid nights apartment dwellers in the Bronx, my father and I included, found it difficult to fall asleep.

On many such nights I remember taking my blanket and pillow and setting them out on the fire escape to escape the heat. The blanket provided scant cushioning against the fire escape's rigid strips of steel. My father would climb out of our bed to keep me company. I would be stretched out on the fire escape and my father would sit on the window ledge, on his pillow, with his back propped up against the window jamb while his legs, bent at the knees, rested on the windowsill. Wearing only our underwear, my father and I would talk for a while and then maybe one of us would temporarily drop off to sleep. Usually, by about two in the morning, the air would cool off and both of us would climb back into bed to finish our interrupted sleep.

After graduation from high school, in June, 1951, I had no idea what to do with myself. I was totally unprepared for the transformation that changed my status overnight from student to adult. It was a shock to my system. It didn't take me long to realize that I was ill-equipped to enter the adult world, complete with full-time employment, and the responsibility of taking care of myself.

By the end of July I realized I needed to get a job of some kind to earn money. My work experience consisted of a few summer jobs, one as a "runner" (messenger) on Wall Street, another as a delivery boy for the U.S. Buckle and Belt Company in the garment district. The company was owned by two Jews. In addition to delivering packages of belt buckles during the day, it was also my responsibility to sweep the floor before quitting time. At the end of my first day I began sweeping. I had not been sweeping very long when one of the owners grabbed the broom from my hand and said, "That's no way to sweep. Watch me. I'll show you how to sweep a floor. See, you got to get under the tables and in the corners." Then he handed the broom back to me. I must say, I was very impressed with his pedagogical demonstration. I remember saying to myself, "This man knows how to sweep a floor." It was a lesson that has stood me in good stead throughout my life.

Another summer job I had was changing flat tires at Ben's Auto Supply Parts near Gun Hill Road. I also had a part-time job after school as a soda jerk at the candy store beneath our building, and I clerked at a dry cleaning store in my neighborhood. At closing time on Saturdays at the dry cleaners, Henry, the presser, a handsome, good-natured, well-built black man, would remove a customer's suit in his size from the racks and would wear it all weekend. Come Monday morning he would press the garment and return it to the racks. I'm sure women considered him to be the best-dressed man in his neighborhood. No one at the cleaners knew his secret but me.

Out of desperation I answered a classified ad as a door-to-door salesman, even though the ad didn't specify what kind of merchandise or service was to be sold. The address given in the ad was on Arthur Avenue (Little Italy in the Bronx). A hand-written sign on the downstairs door advised candidates for the job to proceed up a long flight of stairs. At the top of the stairs I entered a large room—dusty, airless and virtually barren, save for one old desk and several rows of collapsible wooden chairs. In addition to the man seated at the desk, there were about fifteen men, not boys, seated in the chairs. I joined the men in the chairs and listened to the man at the desk address his audience. After a few minutes I discovered that these old guys and I were supposed to sell religious articles: medals to be worn around the neck and miniature statues of various Catholic saints, including Saint Christopher, the patron saint of travelers, designed to sit on the dashboard of an automobile to protect the driver from accidents. Another statue offered for sale was that of saint so-and-so (I forget his or her name) to protect people from sickness. I had the most success selling a glow-in-the-dark statue of a particular saint which was intended to sit on top of a TV set to help improve reception. Included in our portable display case were any number of rosary beads, and a handsome crucifix carved out of rosewood with a se-cret compartment containing holy water allegedly blessed by the Pope. I can only imagine where the water came from!

Many of the middle-aged salesmen in the room could speak other languages—mostly Italian and Polish. Every morning we would assemble at the office, where we were instructed to travel together in one car to a particular neighborhood that hadn't been canvassed recently. I was surprised by how easy it was to sell these religious articles, mostly to mothers and grandmothers, who were home alone during the day in the blue-collar neighborhoods we covered. Their religious sympathies and faith made it difficult for these devout women to turn us down. You could always get them to buy something, even if it wasn't the most expensive item displayed in our portable showcase. To make it as easy as possible to close a sale, we told the woman of the house she had only to put down a small down payment and agree to pay the balance in modest monthly installments. It was almost impossible for them to refuse such generous terms in order to own one of these precious religious objects.

After a few weeks on the job I discovered that the company I worked for sold these installment notes to a collection agency, which would subsequently hound and harass these poor victims to come up with the full payment or pay interest on their debt. By this time the entire enterprise was leaving a bad taste in my mouth, so I quit. As an act of redemption for having taken advantage of these vulnerable women I did not return my sample showcase of religious articles. Instead, I richly enjoyed distributing my samples as gifts to the mothers of my Italian friends.

In 1950, the North Korean army crossed the 38th parallel into South Korea, instigating a bloody conflict that was to last several years and resulting in 33,629 Americans killed in battle, and as many as two million civilian dead. For the first time in my life, I was affected in a personal way by a world event that I felt no connection to. Nor did I feel a patriotic duty to defend my country in a remote place that I had difficulty locating on a map. I had spent my childhood in the blue-collar confines of the Bronx, and had never bothered to cultivate an understanding of the world beyond my neighborhood. I think I was like most kids, and many adults at the time, who felt that World War II had put an end to all future wars. It was inconceivable to me that anyone in their right mind would want to start another war just five years after World War II had ended. Hadn't the world witnessed enough carnage? People around the world were just beginning to dig themselves and their countries out of the rubble of destruction. In America, expectations were high. It was a brand new world, with limitless opportunities for prosperity and happiness. It was time to fall in love, get married and have children. Going to war again didn't make any sense to me.

I was vaguely aware of the Soviet Union's master plan to spread its brand of communism across the world. But I didn't think of the "cold war" as a real war. Maybe I was naïve, but I never believed that the blustering Soviet Union would actually start a nuclear war with the United States over Korea. Needless to say, when war broke out in Korea I was surprised, disappointed and most of all annoyed that I had to serve my country at a time when my adult life was about to begin—not that I had any clear-cut plans for myself. But the idea of leaving New York to fight a war half way around the world did not appeal to me. For one thing, the conflict in Korea didn't seem like the same kind of threat to civilization that Nazi Germany had posed a few years earlier. I felt World War II had been a necessary and moral war that I would gladly have volunteered for. However, I do remember feeling that the United States had to draw the line in the sand some place if it was going to prevent the further spread of communism, and I figured this was perhaps as good as place as any to take a stand, especially after the imperious General Douglas MacArthur assured the American people that he could defeat the north Korean army quickly "with one arm tied behind my back." Despite his boastfulness and his strategic victory at Inchon, the war with Korea quickly became unpopular with the American people. By January 1951,only 38 percent of the public supported the intervention. By November 1952, it had dipped to 23 percent; two out of every three Americans believed the United States should pull its troops out of Korea, and by this time, given the stalemate over there, I was one of them. With no victory in sight on either side, the war ended out of fatigue on July 27, 1953, not with a peace treaty but a cease-fire agreement. I was aboard ship, the LSMR 14, when I heard the news. It was broadcast over the ship's loudspeaker system: "Now hear this. Now hear this. The war in Korea has just ended."

With the outbreak of hostilities in Korea, the government reinstated the draft. Since I was unemployed at the time, military service was a consideration for me. Wanting to avoid the very real possibility of being sent into combat against an enemy I thought was probably as uncivilized and beastly as the Japanese had been in World War II, I decided, along with several of my Bronx buddies, to enlist in the Navy. At the time this seemed like a sensible way to serve my country. Needless to say, my enlistment disrupted my aimless, carefree life—but in retrospect it yielded dividends I could hardly have imagined; it uprooted me from my provincial existence and introduced me to places and people I would never otherwise have come into contact with.

On November 2, 1951, I left New York for the first time in my life and headed for Bainbridge, Maryland, for boot camp. This marked the beginning of my education.

Leaving home created a deep and painful conflict within me. Whether I decided to enter the Army or the Navy, either choice meant leaving my father by himself. I knew this would not be an easy time for him. He was sixty-five at the time, and I knew he would miss me terribly. I could empathize with him later in my own life, when I was sixty-five and had been living by myself for almost twenty years after my divorce. It was a lonely, depressing time in my life and I hated it. Yet I have to admit, there was something about living alone that appealed to the solitary-side of my nature, and that gave me the opportunity to experience what my father had experienced , and somehow this made me feel closer to him.

On the morning that I left for boot camp, I took only a small bag containing a toothbrush, razor and comb. Without saying anything directly, my father and I both understood the implications of my leaving. We said our good-byes at the front door to our apartment. My father was his usual stoic self. No tears. No tentative impulse to reach out for an embrace. No show of any kind of emotion. Not even a handshake. Just a silent understanding between father and son that this was something that had to be done and there was nothing either one of us could do about it.

The night before I left, however, my father told me he thought my military experience would be good for me. He implied that it would "broaden my horizons," although he didn't use those exact words. By getting away from the Bronx he felt

I would have a chance to see different parts of the world and make new friends, the way he did when he was a young man. In looking back, I think my father was waiting patiently for me to grow up.

At the mention of the word "patience," I am reminded of the following tale from the body of instructive Jewish humor:

In Russia, at the beginning of the last century, there was a peddler from Kiev. He found himself in a small town on a Friday night without a place to sleep, and since he didn't want to offend anyone by traveling on the Sabbath, he asked around if anyone knew of a place where he could spend the night. One of the merchants in town suggested he visit the house of a wealthy, religious Jew: he's a very generous man, and I'm sure he'll take you in. So the peddler went to the house and explained his predicament. The man told him there was room in the barn, and that after he got settled he should come to the house and join he and his family for dinner. The peddler could not believe his good fortune that such an important man in the community would be so gracious to a peddler. Seated at the head of the table the man engaged the peddler in conversation. He asked where he came from, did he have a family and children, what kind of wares did he sell. He finally got around to the question of faith, and was shocked when the peddler told him he was not religious and didn't believe in God. When the man heard this, he became furious that such a heathen was seated at his table. The man quickly lost his temper and ordered the peddler from his house. The next morning the man could hardly wait to get to *shul* to tell God what transpired. He was certain God would be pleased with the way he had ushered the non-believer from his home.

When the man finished telling God his story, God answered him and said: "I've been patient with that man for thirty years, and *you* couldn't have patience with him for one hour."

My father's patience notwithstanding, I had no short-term or long-term plans that would enable me to earn a decent living. And it was this, the ability to earn a living, that was for him the most fundamental benchmark of manhood. I think he felt that it was worth the hardship of living alone for the next four years if it would help steer me in the right direction; to make a man out of me. And he was right. My tour of duty in the Navy changed the course of my life. During my absence I wrote to him often and he always replied in penmanship that was uniquely his own—half script, half printed block letters. I'm sorry now I didn't save any of his letters.

Chapter Twenty-Seven

After spending about a year on my first ship, the LSMR 514, (in Little Creek, Virginia), I was somehow plucked from the ranks of the "deck apes," and assigned to be a quartermaster. I cannot recall how this bit of luck came my way, but I was grateful I no longer had to get down on my hands and knees every day and use a hammer and wire brush to remove rust from the ship's decks and hull. As a quartermaster, along with two other more senior quartermasters, it was our job to assist officers by sending and receiving Morse code messages using semaphore flags, signal lights, or by hoisting international flags. Additionally, it was our responsibility to store nautical charts, maps and navigational instruments, all of which I learned to do during a twelve-week course at a naval school in Baltimore, Maryland. Although I managed to graduate, I knew I was not as proficient as most other students in the class. I still did not know how to take class notes or study for exams. These skills would come later. What I did know was that, if I were the captain of a ship, I would never place quartermaster respon-sibilities in the hands of someone like me. To me it was all a game. I didn't take the job seriously, which eventually caught up with me with disastrous results—disastrous for the captain of my ship, that is, not for me.

The disastrous, or comic, event, depending on how you look at it, occurred while our ship was en route to the Caribbean for a series of war games. We were part of a six- ship convoy. Here's how I remember the incident.

It was lunchtime on a crystal clear, sunny day. I was shar-ing the watch with one of the junior officers. It was our job to keep an eye out for any signals coming from the flagship that might require us to change course or initiate some other tacti-cal maneuver. At one point the officer and I noticed that the flagship had hoisted several flags on the ship's halyard. It was my job to identify the various flags and decode them as quickly as possible by referring to a large black book. I was under a great deal of pressure from the officer in charge who kept prod-ding me to hurry up. As it turned out, I either didn't identify the flags correctly using a pair of binoculars, or I didn't decode them properly. In my eagerness to provide him with an answer as quickly as possible, I mistakenly told him the code signal in-structed us to "make smoke," a tactic used to produce a trail of smoke from the stern of the ship to keep us hidden from enemy aircraft in case of an air attack. So the officer gave the order to "make smoke." In the meantime, all the other ships in the squadron correctly, and in unison, made a perfectly ex-ecuted ninety degree turn to the right. We, on the other hand, kept steaming straight ahead. Within seconds the captain of our ship, who was a career officer looking to rise in the ranks, was on the bridge. He knew something was wrong when the wardroom where he was having lunch, along with the galley where the crew was eating, filled up with smoke from a malfunction in the smoke-making equipment. As soon as he observed that we were the only ship not following orders, he directed his frustration at me—for which I could hardly blame him. Eyes blazing with rage, he gave me a thorough dressing down, and dismissed me from the bridge. "Get this man out of my sight," he barked, or words to that effect. There was some scuttlebutt about a court martial but I never heard any more about it.

Did I learn a lesson from this experience? Maybe, at some deeper level that I was not aware of at the time, but on the surface I remained calm and unaffected and, to tell the truth, slightly amused by the entire episode. In looking back on this incident, it seems to me this fiasco could easily have occurred in the TV sitcom *McHale's Navy*. Obviously, I was still not ready to take life seriously, other than caring for and worrying about my father, which brought on migraine headaches—a debilitating malady I suffered until I was released from the Navy and returned home to begin college.

Did I say college? This is probably as much of a surprise to you, dear reader, as it was to me. Let me tell you how it came to pass that I, this uninquisitive, unambitious, unripened kid, even came to consider going to college.

After my time spent serving on the LSMR 514 I was transferred to the troop ship U.S.S. Latimer, where I got to know a fellow named Jim (whose last name I can no longer recall). In addition to his regular duties aboard ship as Yeoman Second

Class, he was also in charge of the ship's library, a resource I didn't even know existed before I met him. Jim was from the Midwest and had attended Ohio State University for several years before enlisting in the Navy. I think he assumed that, like him, everyone read for pleasure or edification, so he asked what books I had read and who my favorite authors were. The moment he asked this question I felt the same sense of doom that I had experienced in elementary school when my music teacher asked me to stand up in front of my classmates and play Adeste Fideles on the clarinet. I felt embarrassed—that time by my musical ignorance, and this time by my literary ignorance. He was appalled when I confessed that I had never read a single book . He offered to remedy the situation by preparing a reading list for me.

His question also caused me to wonder why he had thought I was a reader. This was not the first time someone had assumed I was well read or, at the very least, had some acquaintance with books, or that I was college educated. A few weeks prior to this conversation with Jim I had been sharing the midnight watch with an officer. Because there is not much to do at this hour, we passed the time in conversation. At one point the officer, Ensign Skinner, asked me where I had gone to school. I was smart enough to know he was not asking what high school I had attended. I told him I hadn't gone to college. He said, "Oh, I just assumed you had." This struck me as odd. Here, too, I wondered why he had assumed I had gone to college. His comment altered my thinking. For the first time in my life I wondered if I had what it took to succeed at college.

I was twenty years old when I read my first book, the very first one on Jim's list. It was *Kings Row*, a popular novel written in 1940 by Henry Bellamann. It was a story about an aspiring doctor from a small Midwestern town at the turn of the century who treats his best friend, Drake McHugh, after he loses his inheritance and both his legs in a tragic accident. The second book I read, *The Silver Chalice*, was written by Thomas B. Costain and published in 1952. It was an historical novel depicting the lives of early Christians living in Antioch, Rome and Jerusalem. The story revolves around the search for the Holy Grail.

At the time I had no way of knowing whether these novels were any good from a literary perspective. All I knew was that I couldn't put them down. I was now eager to read the rest of the books on Jim's list. I felt that the characters in these stories were much more real and believable than the characters I was used to seeing in the movies, as much as I loved them. Jim had wisely started me off with accessible page-turners, and I was hooked. Both books had exposed me to places and periods of history I knew nothing about. Not only was I awakened to the pleasure of reading, but for the first time in my life I came face-to-face with the extent of my ignorance. As a result of this insight, I experienced a thirst to learn—to read everything I could get my hands on. Over time, my reading preference shifted to non-fiction, particularly toward history and biographies, because stories about real events and the struggles of real people, were more compelling to me than the best fiction.

As a result of this experience, and many more to follow, it dawned on me that in this life we may come in contact with good role models and bad role models. The good role models inspire us. The bad ones teach us.

Near the end of my four-year enlistment period I found

out— I think when my sister wrote to me about it—that my father, then sixty-nine and still working every day, had suffered several heart attacks, or near heart attacks, or digestive problems compounded by stress that could mimic symptoms similar to heart attacks. As soon as I learned of his trips to the hospital, I applied for a "hardship transfer" so I could be stationed near home to take care of him. The Navy approved my request and reassigned me to a naval base in Bayonne, New Jersey, close enough so I could drive home every evening in the blue 1949 Dodge my father bought me. There was no recurrence of heart attacks or any other ailment after this that I can remember. I took advantage of this opportunity to enroll in a high school remedial English class offered two nights a week at Roosevelt High School on Fordham Road. Then I requested that the Navy release me several months early so I could begin college at New York University in the fall of 1955. My poor study habits produced stammering beginnings, but I managed to finish up three-and-a-half years later with decent grades.

During my college years I would often take a break from studying and enjoy Friday nights with my father watching boxing on TV. Boxing during the 1950s became increasingly popular (second only to baseball) thanks in large measure to two events: (1) The end of World War II which brought veterans back home and many of them back into the ring. (2) The introduction of television into people's homes allowing them to watch a variety of sports events. And boxing was right up there at the top of the list with live broadcasts of the Gillette Friday Night Fights, which proved to be one of the most popular television series in American sports history.

On these Friday nights my father and I would sit next to each other on the couch in our small front room. We would get excited when we heard the voice of commentator Jimmy Powers, and then listen to the catchy Gillette Razor theme song, "Look sharp/Be sharp march." Week after week we watched a lot of low-ranked fighters, but we also saw some outstanding fighters, many of them making a name for themselves in the second half of the 1940s, like Tony Zale and Rocky Graziano who fought each other several times in what fight critics call one of the fiercest rivalries in boxing history. The following morning, after one of their brutal fights, the back page of the New York Daily News would invariably carry a close-up photo, taken at ringside, of one of the fighters receiving a smashing blow to his misshapen face. Other top-notch fighters of the 1940s and '50s included Sugar Ray Robinson, Carmen Basillio, Kid Gavilan, Gene Fullmer, Tony De Marco, Jake La Motta, Floyd Patterson, Willie Pep, Sandy Saddler, Ezzard Charles and many more. I remember how intensely my father watched the fights, and how, every once in a while, his right arm would jerk involuntarily as though he were throwing a hard right punch to the fighter's head or stomach.

When I was in high school, my father and I would occasionally arm wrestle at the kitchen table. Despite my father's age I could never win, until one day, after my discharge from the Navy, the balance of power shifted in my favor. Enjoying good health and high spirits since my return home, my father challenged me to a match. It was touch and go for a minute or so before I sensed his muscles slacken, and all of a sudden I found myself overpowering him. At this point I pinned his arm to the kitchen table. This was the first time I had ever scored a victory over my father. When the match was over we just kind of looked at each other. After a few seconds of awkward silence, I got up from the table and said I had some studying to do. He didn't answer me, but we never arm wrestled again. We both knew something had happened that we didn't have the words to describe, but that had changed forever our father-son relationship.

Chapter Twenty-Eight

In 1957, about a year before I graduated from college with a degree in journalism, I began to reflect on my relationship with my sister. What I realized was that I really didn't have a relationship with her. From 1941 to 1945 I lived in New Rochelle. In 1945, when my father and I moved to the Bronx, I continued to see my sister irregularly on Sundays when my father and I would either visit her in Sea Gate, or meet her in Manhattan for lunch and a movie. After I graduated from high school in 1951 I enlisted in the Navy and was away from New York for the next four years, until 1955, the year my sister moved to Denver. All in all, we had a rather distant relationship for more than sixteen years, at which time I decided to do something to correct the situation. So I called my sister and told her I would like to come out to Denver for a visit. I don't remember what we talked about, but it was a fructifying experience, because after my visit I felt we had embarked upon a new adult sister-brother relationship that brought us closer together, and we and our respective families have remained close ever since.

On several different occasions, around 1966, when my sister's children, Andrew and Shelli, were about five or six, her entire family came to visit my wife and I in New Rochelle. A few years later, both our families, with all four children, met in Washington, DC, to tour the city during summer vacation. On at least one occasion, when I was still married to my first wife, we took our daughters to Denver to celebrate Thanksgiving with my sister and her family. This must have been around 1970. After my divorce in 1980, I traveled to Denver regularly, sometimes with my daughter, Tracy, to celebrate Thanksgiving. Julie was already a principal dancer with the Oakland Ballet, and was usually on tour at this time of year and couldn't be with us. After Tracy married, she and her husband, David, and my two grandchildren, Tristan and Ariana, joined me on my annual trip to Denver for the Thanksgiving holiday. Around the mid-1980s, Andrew and Shelli had moved to San Francisco and both of them, at different times, had come to work for me until they got themselves settled. By 2001 Jean had moved in with me, so we started having our Thanksgiving reunion at our house. It was more efficient for my sister and her husband to come to the Bay Area for Thanksgiving than for all of us to troop off to Denver. After one of her Thanksgiving visits to our home, my sister sent me a "Thank You" card with the following note: "Thank you for opening your home and your heart. You are a most kind and thoughtful person. Just wanted to let you know how much I think of you and how proud I am to have you for a brother."

Back now to my education. To help support myself during my first few years at NYU, I worked part-time at Brooks Brothers and later on as a page at NBC Studios, and after that writing extracts for a small business publication describing new products of every description being introduced in Europe that might be of interest to American companies.

In my last year of college, the journalism department offered me the job of managing the "morgue" —the on-campus reference library where news articles were clipped and archived by hand (in the days before computers). This, along with the money I received from the G. I. Bill, eased my financial burden. As part of my responsibility, in addition to reading the complete New York Times every day of the week, and filing virtually every story in its appropriate manila folder, I also had to check the wire services of the Associated Press (A.P.), United Press (U.P.) and International News Service (I.N.S.) for additional news stories.

As a result of my work in the "morgue," I was offered the opportunity to write a five-minute science news segment for a new NBC Network radio program called *The Sound of Science.* The show was being created in partnership with NYU's Journalism Department. Naturally, I jumped at the opportunity. During the week I would gather as many science-related news stories as I could find and rewrite them for the show. On Friday afternoon I would take the subway to the NBC studios at Rockefeller Plaza and turn in my script to Ben Grauer, one of NBC's legendary commentators and newscasters. The program aired on Sunday afternoons. The first week the show was on the air I listened to it in the kitchen with my father. At the conclusion of the program the announcer said, "The science news portion of the preceding program was compiled and written by Steve Zimmerman." My father turned to me and asked, with a mixture of pride and astonishment in his voice, "Where did you learn to write like that?"

Near the end of my senior year, my favorite Journalism Professor, Sid Towne, an ex-newspaperman, told me there was a scholarship open at Boston University for a master's degree in communications. He asked me if I would be interested. It was tuition free and carried a monthly stipend. All I had to do, along with two other graduate students from other parts of the country, was operate the school's educational radio station (WBUR) during the year while working on my degree. It was professor Towne who gave me the following advice about writing news stories: "When you come to the end, stop." And that, as I later discovered, also applies to many other things in life.

I remember feeling very conflicted about Professor Towne's offer. My ambition was at war with my conscience. On the one hand, I desperately wanted to accept the scholarship and further my education. On the other hand I didn't want to leave my father again. I could see he was slowing down and looking even more tired than usual. I felt terribly guilty. I knew that if I stayed near home I could look after him. Compounding my guilt was a gut feeling, a premonition of sorts, that if I left home to go to Boston there was a good chance I might never see him alive again. Something in me finally decided that I should go to Boston, partly because I felt it was what my father would have wanted me to do. Whether true or not, it helped me make the decision. I reasoned that my father had devoted his life to raising me, to preparing me, as best he could, to be self-sufficient, or in his words, "to stand on my own two feet." I felt that going to Boston to continue my education would be his success as much as mine. To this day I have doubts and regrets about my decision, but no regrets about how I said good-bye to him. I forget the exact words I used, but when my words trailed off I reached out and wrapped my arms around his shoulders and brought him to me in a tight, warm embrace. "I'll miss you, pop," I said, then I walked out of his life.

When I arrived at Boston University in 1958 there were still large gaps in my education, and one of these gaps was classical music—which was not commonly listened to by me or my friends when I was growing up in the Bronx. Nevertheless, it was part of my job at WBUR to emcee a classical music program several nights a week for the station's dedicated classical music lovers. As the show's host I was narrowly able to get by on the air thanks to a music appreciation class I had taken at NYU. At the very least I was familiar with the names of most of the musical giants: Mozart, Beethoven, Brahms, Rachmaninoff, Bach, Tchaikovsky, and so on. By the end of the year my knowledge of classical music had expanded dramatically and I formed a lifelong fondness for many of the pieces I played. The first piece I fell in love with was Grieg's piano concerto in A minor. Being new to this field, however, I didn't pay close attention to the names of newer artists like Van Cliburn, the American pianist who achieved worldwide recognition that year when he won the first International Tchaikovsky Piano Competition in Moscow. My ignorance led to an on-air gaffe.

One evening when I was hosting my classical music program, I chose to play one of Cliburn's recorded pieces. As I proceeded to introduce him over the air, I was turning the record album front to back trying to locate his full name. In my ignorance, I thought "Van" was either his middle name or part of his last name. The only names I could recall on the spot with a name like that were those I remembered from 1930s depression-era movies in which snooty rich people showed up for breakfast attired in formal evening clothes .They had names like Sir Arthur van Pelt, or Lord Reginald van Bonneville, etc . I was certain that Van Cliburn must have had a first name which I was determined to find in the liner notes on the album jacket. When I felt I could no longer keep my audience waiting to hear his performance, I finally blurted out, "And here he is, Harold Van Cliburn." Either no one was listening to my broadcast, or they were too busy laughing to call the station to correct my mistake. Had I been able to think of the actor Van Johnson I might have saved myself from this blunder.

To make matters worse, I addressed my Boston radio audience with a heavy Bronx accent. Fortunately for me, the school administrators had not heard me speak before they awarded me the scholarship. I thought it was laughable to let me broadcast on the air—about as laughable as when Hollywood cast Tony Curtis (born Bernard Schwartz), a fellow Bronxite, to play the part of a Roman slave in *Spartacus* (d: Stanley Kubrick,1960) alongside Kirk Douglas and Laurence Olivier. This was one more misadventure in my young life, but I, once again, managed to escape unscathed, this time with my master's degree in hand.

Three significant events occurred around my move to Boston. The first was my sister's marriage to Sig Rosenfeld, a geologist for Shell Oil Company whom she met in Denver where she was working as a statistician forecasting commodity prices for the U. S. Department of Agriculture. She and Sig met in September, 1958 at the Jewish Community Center, while both were serving on a committee to plan a St. Valentine's Day dinner and dance. They were married May 2, 1959 in Denver in a small ceremony at Temple Emanuel attended by about thirty of their close friends and co-workers. The only family member to attend was Sig's cousin, Irene, a professor at the University of Wyoming. After their honeymoon in Mexico the wedding couple came to New York and celebrated their marriage at a family dinner party hosted by Aunt Frieda in her home in Bensonhurst, Brooklyn. Since I was in Boston at the time, there is a good chance I didn't attend this party because neither I nor my sister have any recollection of my being there. Aunt Frieda probably invited my father, but he may have declined because it would have been a long trip from the Bronx. He may also have turned down the invitation because of the uncongenial relationship he had with her husband, Uncle Lou. My sister and Sig met my father in Manhattan for a short visit before they headed back to Denver. It must have pleased him to see his daughter married with a prosperous future. One less thing for him to worry about at his age. It was also a timely visit, considering that my father died one month later.

The second significant event occurred several months before I left for Boston when I had decided to get married to the girl from the Bronx I mentioned earlier—the one I had met in one of my journalism classes. It was a small wedding in the ground-floor apartment of the Reverend (rabbi) Jerome H. Kallenberg at 4025 Grand Concourse. Of the twenty or so guests, only four were from my family: my father, my sister, and my Aunt Estelle and Uncle Fred—relatives from my father's side of the family. A few of my close friends also attended.

The rest of the guests were from my wife's family because, as my mother-in-law informed me, weddings were not for the people getting married, but for the family, especially for the proud parents—although in this case I don't think that my mother-in-law was too proud of her daughter's choice. On more than one occasion she told her that I was from the wrong side of the tracks. Over the years my mother-in-law would make similar insinuations that nettled me and invariably left me speechless. The wedding reception she (and she alone) arranged, was carried out in impeccably bad taste. It took place in the back room of Siegel's Restaurant, essentially a Jewish deli, located at 45 East 167th Street in the Bronx, six blocks from the old Yankee Stadium. To hear my mother-in-law tell it, you'd think the deli was a four-star restaurant and the dinner a grand affair. Mr. Siegel, the owner, proudly referred to the back room of his deli as his "Banquet Hall." To his credit, he made certain all the guests left his restaurant stuffed to the gills. If I had to summarize my wedding reception, I would say it was an artistic failure but a financial success, thanks to the generous amounts of cash and checks stuffed into my pockets courtesy of the guests.

As discussed earlier, my marriage got off to a rocky start and only got worse as time went on. Contributing to my unhappiness was my poor addle-headed mother-in-law, who, at the invitation of my wife (who did not consult me in the matter) came to live with us on three separate occasions—the first time was after her husband died and left her penniless. On each of these occasions, after several months of living with this vacuous woman, I had to threaten my wife with desertion if her mother didn't leave. To give you a precise sense of my ex-mother-in-law's inanity, it might help if I described the gifts she gave me on two different Christmases. On one occasion she presented me with a bag of Sunsweet dried prunes because, as she said, "I know you like them." It's true. I do like dried prunes. But as a Christmas present? For Christmas in 1973 she gave me a simulated leather appointment book with calendar dates on each page. Initially I thought this was considerate of her until I noticed that the book was for the previous year, 1972, which she undoubtedly purchased at a discounted price. When I brought this fact to her attention, assuming it had been an oversight, she said she knew the calendar was a year old but said that it was still usable since it was only off by a day or two each month. Her explanation reminded me of something Gracie Allen might have said to George Burns. Additionally, she could easily have been the inspiration for the following old comedy routine:

Salesman: "Madam, this vacuum cleaner will cut your work in half."
Customer: "Great! Give me two of them."

After graduating from Boston University in 1959, my wife and I returned to New York where I worked at several different jobs in the sales promotion and advertising fields, before accepting a position with the Pepsi-Cola company in 1971 as Marketing Director for their Foodservice division. In 1974 I resigned from Pepsi and moved to San Francisco to open my own advertising and sales promotion agency (with an office in New York run by my partner, Ira Bernstein, a fellow Bronxite, and the best business partner a guy could ask for). I thought this cross-country move would allow me to escape the proximity of my mother-in-law who, at this point, was living with her adult son, whom she waited on excessively, bringing him his meals in bed. No such luck. After one year in California my wife, for the third and final time, invited her mother to come live with us—once again without consulting me. I had recently purchased a four-bedroom home in Piedmont, California, which had a spare bedroom downstairs that my wife thought would be perfect for her mother. One of the infuriating aspects of having her live with us, for myself and my teenage daughters, was that she wandered around the house in her nightgown, with a cigarette dangling from her lips, until mid-afternoon. It took her that long to get herself organized to the point where she could get herself dressed. I am by nature an even-tempered person and not given to fits of rage, but we all have our breaking point. I reached such a point on one occasion which, remarkably, had no affect whatsoever on either my wife or my mother-in-law, but produced, at least for me, a moment of off-the-wall hilarity.

I returned home from work one day and my mother-in-law was sitting in the living room in one of our comfortable chairs. My wife was sitting on the couch near her. I don't recall exactly what set me off, but I remember leaning over the chair, with both arms resting on either side of her, and looking directly into her face—only inches away from mine. I was yelling at the top of my lungs. I DON'T WANT YOU HERE. YOU'RE RUINING MY LIFE. YOU'RE RUINING

MY CHILDRENS' LIVES. I WANT YOU TO LEAVE THIS MINUTE. I WANT YOU OUT OF THIS HOUSE, NOW." The moment I completed my verbal tempest she looked up at me and said calmly, "Stephen, if I thought you really meant that I would leave."

This was one of those moments where if I had had a gun I would have considered shooting her, but instead I responded to her with disbelief, and like a dithering idiot I wandered off shaking my head. Then I started to laugh because it struck me that this bit of lunacy would make a wonderful movie scene. I could see Shelley Winters playing the part of the Jewish mother. Not long after, her son moved to California, only five minutes from our house. At my insistence, she moved in with him. A few years later, when my daughters were ready, or almost ready, to leave home to be on their own—one to marry and pursue her career as a dancer with Oakland Ballet, and the other to leave for college—I walked out the front door of our house, never to return.

Chapter Twenty-Nine

In 2012 I had a telephone conversation with my sister and discovered something about my father I had never known. While speaking to her I told her about a childhood incident that lingered at the far reaches of my memory, and asked her if she could shed any light on it.

I think I must have been seven or eight at the time when my father took me to visit a woman in her apartment in the Bronx. When I asked him where we were going he said, "To visit one of your mother's friends." I remember this woman as having a sweet face and a warm, pleasant smile. I remember, too, that she had a soft, melodious voice, and that her apartment was spotlessly clean and comfortably furnished. It had a homey feel to it. As young as I was, I was able to sense that my father had arranged this visit because he wanted the two of us to meet—to look each other over, to see how we got along. Sometime during our visit the thought crossed my mind that perhaps my father was thinking of making this woman my new mother. I was not disturbed by this thought because I liked her.

When I told my sister about this visit, she said to me, "Maybe this was the same woman he brought out to Sea Gate for a visit." This was something I had never heard about before. She said she didn't know who the woman was or what she was doing there, and admitted that she was not very friendly toward her. At the time that my father may have been considering remarrying, my sister was quite comfortable living with Aunt Lee. She had many friends in Sea Gate that she would have been reluctant to part with if our father had remarried, which could help explain her admitted coolness toward this woman. Then my sister said something that totally surprised me: "I wish he would have married again. He was such a lonely man." I say surprised because this was the first time I had ever heard my sister speak of our father with any empathy. After we hung up, I thought about what my sister had said, about his getting married again, and I wasn't certain if she meant he should have gotten married then, when she was a youngster, or later on when she was grown up and on her own. At this point in our lives, I feel any questions I may have are better off left unanswered.

Another memory helps fill out this part of the puzzle. Around the time this woman made her appearance in our lives, I distinctly remember my father asking my sister and I the following question: "Would you like it if Daddy got married again?" I do not remember what our response was, but there is a good chance it was not uniformly positive. If that were the case, knowing my father, he would not have gone any further with tentative plans to remarry. In hindsight, I think my father should never have left this decision up to two small children. Speaking for myself, I wish he had married this woman. If she was half as nice as I remember her—that is, at least as nice as Mrs. Cohen— I think I would have had a much happier and more secure childhood, and my father would have had a second chance at happiness.

And now to the third significant event that happened during my year in Boston: the death of my father. At the time of his death he was living in the apartment we had rented after I had been discharged from the Navy and begun my freshman year at NYU. I had found this new place to live because my father had complained that our previous ground-floor apartment (in a two-family home in the Pelham Parkway section of the Bronx) was depressing to him because it was too dark. The new apartment (also in a two-family home), in the quiet working-class Castle Hill section of the Bronx, was upstairs with plenty of sunlight. The street address was 2113 Hermany Avenue. The downstairs apartment was occupied by the owners, the Cannatas, a pleasant, middle-aged Italian couple.

I received news of my father's death by phone from my in-laws at about eight-thirty in the morning just as I was about to leave for school. I immediately made plans to return to New York to make arrangements for my father's funeral. I knew he had reserved a plot for himself next to my mother's grave at Beth David Cemetery in Elmont, Long Island.

The first order of business was to visit the hospital where the ambulance had taken my father so I could officially identify the body. When I arrived, a female receptionist advised me to take the elevator to the basement where the morgue was located. A young, impersonal male orderly was on duty at the time. I told him who I was and gave him my father's name. He left the desk and casually returned a few minutes later with a manila envelope containing my father's personal effects—the things he had in his pockets when he died. In the envelope was the Elgin wristwatch I had given him for his birthday when I was sixteen, a small silver ring in the shape of a turtle shell he wore on his pinky, a roll of Tums, his wallet with his driver's license, his eye glasses, his keys to the house and truck, his pen knife, and a receipt from a local dry cleaners for one pair of gray workmen's trousers. There was no money, not even a few dollars, among his belongings, which I didn't think to question at the time. It didn't make any difference.

The orderly asked me if these were my father's things. I said they were. Then he asked me if I wanted to see the body. I told him "No." I felt it wasn't necessary since I could tell from the articles in the envelope that it was my father. I also felt that I didn't want to inconvenience the attendant by making him go over to a cold storage box where he would have to pull out my father's body and place it on a gurney so I could "view the remains"—a procedure I had witnessed many times on TV and in detective movies.

At this point I placed my father's personal belongings back in the manila envelope and started to leave. But as I reached the swinging doors to exit the morgue I was overcome by a powerful emotion—an intense desire to see my father one last time. I returned to the orderly's desk and told him I had changed my mind. He proceeded to walk me over to a "viewing area" located behind a large, thick plate glass window that began at waist level and rose to the ceiling. A few minutes later the attendant wheeled the steel gurney toward me with my father's body on it. He maneuvered the gurney on the other side of the glass wall which separated me from my father. When I looked down at him he was absolutely motionless under a white sheet that covered his body up to his shoulders. His waxen face wore a peaceful expression. I immediately felt a sense of profound relief; relief for him, knowing that nothing in this world could hurt him anymore. No more painful dental work on his teeth and gums requiring him to wear dentures that never fit properly and caused him great pain when he ate. No more strapping on his cumbersome corset every morning to protect his hernia. No more driving miles and miles every day in sweltering heat with no air conditioning, or during the brutally cold winters when the roads were covered with snow and ice. No more shopping for dinner. No more cooking his own meals and cleaning up afterwards. No more sitting home at night alone with his bottle of beer reading the *World-Telegram & Sun*. No more of anything that would continue to wear him down. He had suffered enough. He had accomplished what he had set out to do—to raise his two children the best he could; the best way he knew how. He had lived to see my sister and I graduate from college, get married and begin our lives, with the promise that we would be able to earn our own way in the world without his help. At age seventy-three he was emotionally worn out. His diseased heart was also worn out. At this point I think he was so tired that he finally permitted himself to rest, to let go of life—to free himself from all obligations and responsibilities—and it was in this sense that I felt relief and happiness for him. As I looked down at his face one last time I could find only stillness and peace there. As best I can tell, he had lived his life with no regrets or need for self-recrimination. He played the cards he was dealt until the game was over. When I felt it was time to leave I said aloud, "Goodbye, Pop. I love you."

My father's death occurred on the morning of June 26, 1959. He had been leaving for work when he collapsed and fell down a flight of stairs. The landlady, Mrs. Cannata, heard the noise and rushed to my father's side. While her husband telephoned for an ambulance she sat next to my father on the steps and cradled him in her soft, generous arms during his final minutes before he lost consciousness and died. I have always been grateful to this woman for the compassion that, hopefully, allowed my father, in those last few moments of his life, to feel the comfort of a woman's arms about him.

About a year later, out of the blue, I was overcome with grief over the loss of my father.

I remember walking into the living room after dinner and sitting down on one of our cushiony chairs. I sank into a state of deep sorrow and began sobbing uncontrollably. My wife must have heard me crying while she was washing the dishes, and walked over to me. At first I thought she had come to comfort me, and I was pleased that she had, that she cared. But she just asked me why I was crying. I told her I missed my father terribly and that this was the first time I had cried over him since his death. She either felt frightened by my outpouring of feelings, or thought I would like to be alone in my grief. Whatever her reason, she turned and left the room without saying a word. At first I was hurt that she hadn't stayed, that she hadn't put her arms around me, or touched me in a comforting way. But once she had gone I felt relieved; I could mourn for my father more fully, more uninhibitedly, if I were alone. I remember I cried for quite awhile, and when I stopped I felt an overwhelming sense of relief. I felt I had unburdened myself of a heaviness I had been carrying around with me for over a year. After a while I got up and went to bed. With my head on the pillow, staring up at the ceiling in the darkness, I remember thinking to myself that I had never cried like that over the loss of my mother.

As I write this at age eighty-two, I remember so many fine qualities about my father: his probity, his self-reliance, his sense of responsibility toward my sister and I, his strength in the face of adversity, his tendency to be of help to others when he could, his consistent patience and understanding, his self-effacing manner, his unflagging concern for my safety and happiness. All of these qualities made up my father, my unlikely hero, and I hope the best of them have become a part of me.

About the author

After his honorable discharge from the Navy in 1955, Zimmerman enrolled at New York University where he earned a B.A. in Journalism. Upon graduation he was awarded a scholarship to do graduate work at Boston University where he earned a master's degree in Communications. Upon returning to New York in 1959, he accepted a position with the Muscular Dystrophy Association as a copywriter and associate producer for the Jerry Lewis telethon. He then took a job as a promotional copywriter for *Look Magazine*. Several years later he went to work for General Foods in the marketing department, where he eventually assumed the position of Promotion Manager for the Kool-Aid division. Wishing to broaden his work experience, he took a job with Grey Advertising in New York as Vice President of merchandising. He left there after several years and took a position with Pepsi-Cola as Marketing Director for their food-service division. He resigned from Pepsi in 1974 to open East West Promotions, a sales promotion and advertising agency, with offices in San Francisco and New York. In 2010 McFarland & Company published his book, *Food in the Movies*, a study of food films and their emergence as a new film genre. In 2013 he retired at age eighty. He lives with his wife in the San Francisco Bay Area.

You may contact the author at: eastwestzim@comcast.net

CPSIA information can be obtained
at www.ICGtesting.com
Printed in the USA
FSHW02n1815050918
51846FS